MAJOR PAIN: CONFESSIONS OF A SMASH-MOUTH SAFETY

Major Wright

Copyright 2020 The Wright Publishing Company LLC

All rights reserved, including the right to reproduce this book or portions thereof in any form whatsoever. For information, address The Wright Publishing Company LLC - P.O. Box 310471 Miami FL 33231

For information about special discounts for bulk purchases or to book an event, please visit our website at www.majorwright.com.

Book Cover designed by CRAYTON Design Co.
Book Cover Photography by Mike Perez
Book Edited by Mike Kennedy

Library of Congress Cataloging-In-Publication Data has been applied for.

ISBN (Paperback): 978-1-7345869-0-9
ISBN (Hardback): 978-1-7345869-1-6
ISBN: eBook: 978-7345869-2-3

Printed in the United States of America

While the author has made every effort to provide accurate Internet addresses and other contact information at the time of publication, neither the publisher nor the author assumes any responsibility for errors or changes that occur after publication. Further, the publisher does not have any control over and does not assume any responsibility for third-party websites and their content. This book is not intended as a substitute for psychological or medical advice. The methods described within this book are the author's personal thoughts. Any use of this information is at your own risk.

TABLE OF CONTENTS

Preface   vii

Chapter 1   Neighborhood Superstar   1
Chapter 2   Moving Daze   6
Chapter 3   Perfectly Positioned   12
Chapter 4   Senior Moments   19
Chapter 5   Starting Time   25
Chapter 6   Living the Dream   31
Chapter 7   Three's a Crowd   38
Chapter 8   The Need for Speed   45
Chapter 9   Bear Necessities   53
Chapter 10   Lessons Learned   60
Chapter 11   Driven to Distraction   68
Chapter 12   The End Zone   76

Epilogue   85

PREFACE

Major, I think you should write a book because you have been going through a lot and have a lot to say that could help others.

Those words came from my ex-girlfriend Laisha Fox, during a late-night phone call in January 2019. They hit me like a ton of bricks—the same way I used to unload on opposing receivers during my 20 years playing football. Isha and I were having an amazing conversation about our goals and what we wanted to accomplish in the future. Isha has her own business, LLF Consulting. She knows something about setting goals and achieving them. She really got me thinking.

The first thing that came to my mind was the book I was reading at the time, *The 15 Invaluable Laws of Growth* by John Maxwell. In his book, Maxwell mentions that the Law of Diminishing Intent says the longer you wait to do something you should do now, the greater the odds that you will never actually do it. I took the opportunity to use that information and see if it really works.

In writing this book, I wanted to create something everyone could relate to, and use the lessons I learned during my football career as a way to help readers make improvements in their own lives. In life, we all face obstacles. Believe it or not, *you* are the true determining factor for overcoming all those challenges. I fully believe that there is nothing in life you can't do, if you are consistent and motivated about it.

I learned this lesson over and over again during my many seasons on the football field. I was first introduced to the sport as an 8-year-old growing up in Florida. Little did I know back then that football would open my life to a world of possibilities I never imagined and expose me to experiences I couldn't find anywhere else. Football also presented struggles that tested me in unexpected ways and pushed me beyond my limits.

For 10 years starting with my freshman season at the University of Florida and then through seven seasons in the NFL, football was my life. I played for a national championship team in college, and won a division title with the Chicago Bears in 2010. As a hard-hitting safety, I loved to lay the wood on opponents. My physical style of play earned me the nickname "Major Pain." I didn't care who you were—a star quarterback or a backup tight end—my presence had to be felt. I developed that mentality super early in my football life, and it carried through my entire career.

But all that ended when my life as a professional football player came to a close. It was a hard transition for me. For the first time ever, I was being told I wasn't good enough to play the sport I loved so much. It was frustrating because I didn't have any control over the situation. I felt lost, empty, and confused. It hurt so bad because I didn't know why I couldn't find another opportunity. There are 32 teams in the NFL, and every one of them has two safeties playing on defense. I couldn't believe there were 64 safeties on the planet better than me.

Dealing with the end of my NFL career drove me into depression. Football was all I had, and I hadn't set myself up for a life after it. I realized I only had myself to blame. I didn't listen to the guidance the NFL gave me during my playing days, and I didn't listen to my mom, who always told me that I needed to look beyond football. She used to say to me that the NFL stands for *Not For Long*. I would get so mad when she would say that, but of course I found that she was so right.

Three years removed from the NFL, and with no job, I got approved for an NFL Line of Duty Disability (or LOD). An LOD provides a short-term benefit to a player for injuries sustained during his career. I played through a lot of pain, especially as a pro. My LOD gave me hope. I felt a little momentum happening. I rediscovered that "little kid" mentality, going for anything I wanted and not letting anything or anyone get in my way.

Soon, I was attacking life the way I used to attack football. I started a backpack company called the Wright BaaGZ and I started my foundation The Wright Way helping single parent moms. I also started working out again. I loved doing it and found it to be great therapy.

In addition, I took Isha's advice and began writing this book. It has been an eye-opening experience. Throughout this process, I learned a lot about myself and how my football career shaped me as a person. My book is for anyone who is facing an obstacle in life. The ability to overcome that obstacle lies within you. At each and every phase of my life, I have faced some type of challenge. And any time I had success, it was because I believed in myself, acted consistently and never quit. I applied the same principles to writing this book. I hope you get as much out of it as I have.

CHAPTER 1
NEIGHBORHOOD SUPERSTAR

I just don't think football is for me.

That was my first thought the first time I played organized football. It was 1996. I was 8-years-old and weighed far below the 75lb. limit. As excited as I was about putting on my pads, I was still nervous about what I had gotten myself into. I remember very distinctly lining up to do the hamburger drill. That's when two players lay on their backs five yards apart. One player is the runner and the other is the tackler. The coach blows the whistle, and both guys jump to their feet as fast as possible. The runner tries to make it past the tackler, while the tackler tries to stop the runner.

On this day, the coach put the ball in my hand and told me I was the runner. When he blew the whistle, I got up on my feet in a flash. So did the other kid, the tackler. He was one of our best players. As I started to run, he came up very fast and hit me super hard. I went down and immediately saw stars. It felt like someone snatched the soul out of me. I cried for a little bit and was completely lost. At that moment, I was thinking that football might not be for me.

That day when I got back home, I told my mom I didn't want to play anymore. She asked me why, and I explained to her about the hamburger drill. I said that I felt like I was about to die after I got hit. My mom wasn't trying to hear it. *Boy, I didn't spend my hard earned money for you to quit. You better go out there and get him back.*

As usual, my mom made her point. I was back on the field the next day, though I did everything in my power to stay away from that kid who knocked me clean off my feet.

My mom, Andrea Eluett, has always had that kind of impact on me. I was born on July 1, 1988, in Fort Lauderdale, Florida, and grew up in a single-parent home. My father, Major Wright, popped in from time to time to check on me, but he was never a consistent influence in my life. I was my parents' oldest child. On my mom's side, it was me and my little sister, Alexus Bryan. On my dad's side, there were four sisters: Charity, Brianna, Tatiana, and Annette and 2 brothers: Majon and Daniel. I grew up in a tough neighborhood called Lauderdale Manors. We lived with my grandmother Carolyn Lee, and her two sons, my uncles Malcolm Lewis and Chris Lee. Chris was only three years older than me, so he was the big brother I didn't have.

My grandfather, Harry Wright, also played a big role in my life. He was a pastor at the Healing Temple Church of Christ in Pompano. We would attend a few times a month. I learned that when you are facing problems or when there is something you want, don't ever be afraid to go to God for it. *Ask and you shall receive. God will never fail you.*

One of my good friends in Lauderdale Manors was Jeffery Harris, who everybody knew as "J-Black." He was the neighborhood football star, and he saw potential in me. J-Black would always tell me that I needed to play. When I would say that I don't know how, he would assure me that the coaches would take care of that. J-Black was a great salesman, constantly talking about winning games, scoring touchdowns, and all the fun he was having out at the parks every Saturday.

Finally, one day J-Black got through to me. I went right home and told my mom I wanted to play football. She was skeptical to say the least. *Boy, you don't know nothing about football. Plus I don't have no money for that right now. But I'll think about it.*

That was all I needed to hear. I ran out of the house straight to J-Black's house and told him that my mom said she was going to sign me up. It was a straight lie, but I was too excited to care. J-Black played for Lauderdale Lakes Vikings, and said that was the team for me.

The following week, J-Black came to my house and bumped into my mother. He mentioned our conversation about the Vikings, and told her how great it would be to have me as teammate. This came as a complete shock to my mom. She called me outside to the front porch, and asked why I had lied. I tried to explain how much I wanted to play football. Then J-Black came to my defense, and convinced my mom to let me give the sport a shot. But instead of the Vikings, she signed me up for a team right across the street, the Western Tigers.

My first year of football was a true learning experience. The coaches put me at second-string offensive guard, a position I knew nothing about. I remember thinking they were so mean. On the second day of practice, they had us do conditioning, running 40-yard sprints. If anyone jumped the whistle, we got an extra one added on. Oh boy, we ended up doing an extra 15 because we were all jumping.

The next day after practice, we did the "six inches" drill. It was the hardest thing I had ever done. In this drill, you lie on your back and raise your legs six inches off the ground on the coach's command. If anyone drops their legs before he says so, you all go back to the beginning and start all over again. Kids were in so much pain they were crying.

After a few days of practice, I went to J-Black and told him that football wasn't any fun. He convinced me to give it more of a chance. *Watch and be patient. It will get better.*

J-Black was right. In fact, in my first season, we won the Super Bowl. I wore #64, and played every bit of 15 snaps. Still, my mom came to see every game. We had a kid named Hammer, who played running back. He was very popular and really good. In the Super Bowl, we faced J-Black and the Vikings. When we beat them, he was so salty. To be honest, I was a bit salty too. I didn't really feel a part of the win because I just sat on the sideline watching my teammates work. I didn't want to feel that way ever again.

Weeks later, I was playing murder-ball with friends outside my Godmother's apartment complex. Murder-ball is a simple game—you tackle whoever has the ball as hard as you can. When I was the runner, no one could touch me. A man watching the action came up to me, and asked if I played for a team. I told him I was a guard for the Western Tigers. He responded that I was clearly on the wrong team and in the wrong position. It turns out he was a coach with Lauderdale Lakes Vikings. He spoke to my mom, and a few days later I was a Viking. I could hardly wait for the 1997 season to start.

The coaches for Lauderdale Lakes saw me as an impact player. They put me at running back and linebacker. I asked for #5, and they gave it to me. As I put on my pads for our first practice, all I could think about was when that kid hit me a year earlier. I never wanted to feel that pain again. So when I ran the ball, it was with the fear of getting hit. That worked really well for me.

Football had never been so much fun. I felt like I had found my identity. We went to the Super Bowl that year, and faced my old team, the Western Tigers. It was a different story this time around. Lauderdale Lakes won, and I was a major contributor. That victory earned us an invite to the Orange Bowl for the state championship. We lost, but it wasn't all bad news. I was named MVP of the game. My mom was super proud of me.

For the 1998 season, I moved up to 95lb. level. I had an even better year, but we lost in the Super Bowl. At that point, my name was ringing around the parks—and in the newspapers. I had replaced J-Black. I was now the new neighborhood superstar. I started to fall in love with the game of football.

CHAPTER 2
MOVING DAZE

*I didn't want to start all over again,
meeting new people and trying to fit in.*

I experienced this feeling on many occasions when I was young. We moved a lot, and I was forced to adjust to new surroundings and make new friends. It wasn't easy, but I never had a choice.

In 2000, after I finished 6th grade, my mom decided to move us to Orlando so she could be with her boyfriend Corey. I wasn't happy about it. My family and all my friends were in Fort Lauderdale. I held this against Corey for several weeks, not speaking to him and going against whatever he said. I felt like he was the reason for our move, so I took it out on him. I was mad at my mom as well, because she could have left me in Fort Lauderdale with my grandmother.

No matter how I felt, I had to get over it quickly. I wanted to play football, and I couldn't do so without my mom and Corey. When I asked her if she would sign me up, she told me to ask Corey. He knew the local parks much better than she did. I built up the courage to ask him, and he agreed, on one condition. *Boy, if I sign you up for football, you better not waste my money.*

The next day Corey came in my room and said we were going to see a team called Pine Hills Trojans. Right there, I started thinking he wasn't that bad of a guy after all. I mean, he was willing to find a team for me *and* pay for it. When we got to the park, Corey talked to the Pine Hills coaches. They looked at me and asked my name, where I was from, and what position I played. I told them I was Major Wright from Lauderdale, and I played running back and linebacker. They giggled and told me that the team already had a pretty good running back. Even though I didn't have my pads yet, I joined my new teammates for non-contact drills. I would get my equipment the following day and practice in full.

On the way home, Corey asked me if I was scared. The question surprised me. *Of what? Them boys? I ain't scared of nothing.*

Or maybe I was, just a little. That night, I couldn't sleep thinking about the next day. I woke up with butterflies in my stomach as if it was game day. I was so excited to show Corey, my coaches, and my teammates what I was made of. When we got to the park, the coaches handed me my equipment and I got fully dressed. The team warmed up all together, and then we moved right into a tackling drill. Coach told us to line up across from someone and form a line. Next, we created a tunnel, reaching our hands up and grabbing those of the teammate across from you. A runner would be stationed at one end of the tunnel and a tackler at the other end.

I was first up as the runner. On the coach's call, I ran through the tunnel full speed and approached the tackler waiting for me at the other end. On pure instinct, I dropped my shoulder and powered right over him and kept going. Everybody got so crunk! The coaches were impressed. I looked over at Corey. He had a huge smile on his face. *That's my stepson!*

From that moment on, I had the total respect of my coaches, teammates and Corey. When we got home, he told my mom that I was the real deal. I ended up starting at running back and linebacker for Pine Hill that season, and made quite a name for myself.

The following year, our family was on the move again, this time back to Fort Lauderdale. I lived with my godmother Yvonne because my mom was taking pharmacy classes at Florida Agricultural and Mechanical University in Tallahassee. I was in 8th grade, and had graduated to the 125lb. level in football. I rejoined Lauderdale Lakes Park in my new weight class. We had another good team, and went all the way to the Super Bowl, though we lost to the Lauderdale Hill Lions. Their top player was Bobby Crawford. He was probably the best running back our league had ever seen. We couldn't stop him for nothing.

Halfway through the school year, my mom decided to move my little sister and I up to Tallahassee with her. I was angry and acted out. I didn't take school seriously. I felt like an easy target for bullies, so I tried to fit in by being the cool new kid on campus. It didn't go very well. In my reading class, this kid named Jimmy took it upon himself to pick on me. He had the whole class laughing at me, calling me all type of names, picking on what I was wearing and calling me soft. I got so mad and told him that I would beat his ass. The class was shocked. Jimmy then told me to meet him across the street after school, *tough guy*. I told him that it wasn't a problem.

For the rest of class, I couldn't stop thinking about the fight. If I didn't show, I would be the laughing stock of the whole school, and everyone would know they could come for me. When the bell rang, it was time for me to either step up or shut up. I saw one of my neighborhood friends, Chad, who had heard about the fight. He told me he had my back if things got out of hand.

When I saw Jimmy, he acted like he didn't want to fight. I couldn't let him off that easy. I picked up a rock and threw it at him. Jimmy was furious and came running towards me. As he got closer, he swung twice, and I dodged both punches. I responded with everything I had, connecting with a right hook that put Jimmy flat on his back. Then I jumped on him and punched him one more time before Chad grabbed me, warning me that the police were on their way. We ran away as fast as we could. This was my first ever serious fight, other than squaring off against my uncle Chris growing up. Honestly, I didn't know what I was doing. It was all reaction and not wanting to be hit.

The next day, I wore a Muhammad Ali outfit to school that my uncle Chris had bought for me. When I got there, the fight was the talk of the whole school. I felt like the big man on campus—you couldn't tell me nothing. In retrospect, there couldn't have been a better first fight than this one. Afterwards, there wasn't any more picking on the new guy. I earned my respect throughout the school.

Still, being in Tallahassee didn't work for me. In fact, I failed in my 8th grade year at R. Frank Nims Middle School. It was the most embarrassing thing I had ever gone through, repeating the same grade because I didn't apply myself. My mom put me on punishment. At first she said it would be for the whole summer, but I ended up doing two weeks. I promised my mom that I would never let anything like that happen again.

The year 2002 was when I got my shit together and locked in. Not just in school, but on the football field as well. But there were still struggles. One day I got a phone call from my father. I was so happy to talk to my pops, but he was calling to tell me that my grandmother Daisy Wright had passed away. I dropped the phone and started screaming. My mom came running to see what was wrong. I told her about Daisy, and we started crying. I loved my grandma. I was her favorite. She spoiled me so much.

After the funeral, things calmed down, but I missed Daisy dearly. I relied on football to help me cope. Being on a team created a lot of relationships for me, but I didn't have to do that much talking to help them along the way. I could make a name for myself with my performance.

The 2002 season was a great one for R. Frank Nims Middle School. We went from worst to first. I also became friends with twin brothers named Keith and Kevin, who lived right across the street from me. Their big brother, Nevin, was a baller for sure. He was just about to head to Hampton University on a full ride. Keith and Kevin went to Bellview Middle School, a team we had played on the way to our championship. They were set to attend Amos P. Godby High School the following year. I was unsure where I was going, and they convinced me to try Godby.

As a freshman in the fall of 2003, I began the season on the Junior Varsity. Keith and Kevin, meanwhile, made the Varsity. I ain't gonna lie. I felt some type of way about that, because I was certain I was every bit as talented as them. But I didn't let that distract me. Instead, I played lights out, scoring six touchdowns in my first three games and leading the team in tackles.

One day, I got called into the office of Varsity coach Sheldon Crews. I wondered what did I do now. Crews looked me in the eye and told me that Godby's starting linebacker was done for the season. As a result, I was being promoted. Crews asked if I wanted to continue to play running back. I paused for a moment, still taking this whole process in. Finally, I said that I would stick with linebacker.

That same day in practice, I assumed I would be playing as a backup, but shockingly they had me running with the starters. I knew the defense because we ran the same scheme on JV, so I was able to fit right in. Was I ready for this? I didn't really know, but I refused to back down. I went out and had a great year, finishing as the fifth leading tackler on the team.

Our linebacker coach at Godby never really liked giving people their props. But at the end of the season, he told me that I was a great player with a bright future ahead of me. I was so happy—and more motivated than ever. After the football season, I chose to run track. Many of my teammates were sprinters, and I knew from them that running track would help me on the football field. I competed in the 100 and 200-yard dash.

By the end of the school year, I was as happy as I had been in a long time. Then I got bad news again. My mom told me that we were moving back to Fort Lauderdale. She needed to go back to do her pharmacy residency. My coaches at Godby were totally caught off guard. They stepped in and tried to arrange for me to stay in Tallahassee with Keith and Kevin and their family. They didn't want to lose one of their best defenders. But my mom was not letting that happen, and I followed her back to Fort Lauderdale.

CHAPTER 3

PERFECTLY POSITIONED

Make every opportunity count.

That was some of the best advice I ever received. It came before a game during my sophomore season as St. Thomas Aquinas High School, from one of the senior receivers, Richard Goodman, who was outworking everyone on the team. Choosing to attend St. Thomas proved to be a smart decision. But it wasn't an easy one.

Before we moved back to Fort Lauderdale in the summer of 2004, I visited my family there and went to the Soul Bowl, a huge game between Dillard High School and Blanche Ely High School. During the game, I ran into Bobby Crawford. He was pumped to see me, and I was pumped to see him. Bobby was going to St. Thomas, and he couldn't stop talking about how big time it was. He definitely got me interested. We exchanged numbers, and he told me to check out the school.

A few weeks later, I was back in Fort Lauderdale, living with my family at my grandmother Carolyn Lee's place in Lauderdale Manors. We had a full house, with me, my sister, my mother, and my two uncles all sharing space. We had three bedrooms and also had to use the living room and den as bedrooms. It was crowded, but we made it work.

Once we were settled, it was time to start looking for my next high school. I remembered my conversation with Bobby and reached out to him about St. Thomas. He told me he would set up a meeting with Coach George Smith. At that time, I really didn't know anything about St. Thomas, only that Bobby went there. When I told some of my neighborhood homies that I might be attending that high school, they were impressed. *Bro, that's a great school. You can make it to college in that school.*

My meeting with Coach Smith went well. Towards the end of it, he asked me two questions: What number would you wear and what position do you play? I picked number 21, because the first player who came to mind was Sean Taylor. He had gone as the fifth pick overall in the NFL Draft earlier that spring after a great career at the University of Miami. I loved the way he played. I also remembered DeAndre McDaniel, a safety at Godby High School, and really liked his style. I decided I was better off playing safety, too. At this point in my career, I realized my body frame and speed were more suited to the secondary.

After the meeting, I went home to talk things over with my mom. She had some concerns about St. Thomas and asked where I wanted to go. I told her I wasn't sure. I knew my mom had attended Boyd H. Anderson High School, and I liked the idea of keeping that tradition going. My cousin Gerald Williams went to B. A., too. He played middle linebacker for the Cobras and was a beast. I hit him up, and he invited me to a workout at the school. In no time, I was running in drills at safety.

A few weeks later, as the deadline to register for school was approaching, I got a call from Coach Smith at St. Thomas. He didn't waste any time. *Major, where the hell are you? Why are you not working out here? Better yet, bring your ass and cleats out here tomorrow.*

I told my mom about the call, and we both knew that St. Thomas was right for me. I also told my cousin. He wasn't happy at all, especially since I had already started working out with B. A. But he understood and wished me well.

My first day of workouts at St. Thomas blew me away. The place was so upscale, and I was amazed at how organized practice was. Seeing all the championships the school had won really shocked me. At that point, I realized why this school was big time.

I won't lie, I was a little shaky during practice. It was my first time at safety, and I was learning on the go. But being home and around family made me comfortable and less stressed out. I knew I didn't have to fit in. I spent a lot of time watching Sean Taylor highlights. I told myself I would be just like him. Weeks passed by and I got the hang of my new position.

When it was time for the pads to come on, I couldn't wait to show my coaches and teammates what I was really about. In our first practice, we started with a kickoff drill. I was put on the cover unit, and our special teams coach instructed us to sprint downfield and make the tackle. When the whistle blew, I took off like I was shot out of a cannon. A player tried to block me, and I ran right through him, and then I took down the returner. The coaches were hyped, but they told me to tone it down. That wasn't how they practiced at St. Thomas. We lined up again, and on the whistle, I did the exact same thing. Ah man, why did I do that? The special teams coach cursed me out, and I told him it was my bad. It was my first dose of being seen as not coachable, and it didn't feel good at all.

For our spring jamboree, we faced Miami Carol City Senior High School. This was Dade County versus Broward County, so there was a lot on the line. At this point, I was an unknown starting at safety, but I was determined to leave this game with everyone asking about #21. My first big play came when the tight end caught a pop pass. I cleaned his clock and sent him to the sideline. The crowd went wild. We ended up beating Carol City. I loved every bit of that feeling and wanted more of it.

Our season opener was against Cardinal Gibbons High School. On the second play of the game, they ran a toss with a pulling guard. I came downhill, blew the guard up, and made the tackle. We were all going nuts on the field. So was the student section in the stands. Our offense struck first, putting us up 7-0. On the next series, the tight end ran a drag route. I read the play, pursued at full speed, and put my shoulder right in his chest, causing him to drop the ball. We defeated Gibbons, 34-13. Everybody had the same reaction about me. *Who is this guy, and where did he come from?*

We wound up finishing the 2004 season at 12-2. Our two losses came against Deerfield Beach High School, and then Lakeland High School in the state championship. That game was played at the University of Florida stadium, nicknamed the Swamp. Man, Lakeland was really good. We couldn't stop their best back, Chris Rainey. He scored four times on us. We were so bad on defense they scored 31 points to our 7. Still, we had come so close to winning a ring.

Despite the loss to Lakeland, I was grateful for being a part of the St. Thomas family. I finished the season with 71 tackles and five interceptions. There was no better feeling than stepping up whenever I was needed.

After the football season, I ran track again. This time around, I added the 4 x 100 relay to my resume. I needed to get faster, so this was the best way to learn the proper running techniques. No doubt about it, my speed increased, thanks partly to learning how to open up my stride.

Going into my junior year, my mindset was to hit everything that was moving and ask questions later. St. Thomas made headlines by adding Hall of Famer Cris Carter as the offensive coordinator. He took me under his wing and gave me excellent advice on what I needed to work on.

Before our 2005 opener, I got great news when I was named a team captain. I was proud to be recognized as a leader. When the season began, we rolled like we always did and raced to a 4-0 start. Then we faced South Broward High School. We went on to beat them 56-7.

Our next game against Deerfield was intense. We expected another dogfight, and they gave us all we could handle, beating us 42-14. It was so sickening to take a loss from them again, but our goal of winning the state championship was still in front of us.

We sat at 7-1, with Western High School up next. In the first quarter, we forced them to punt. I came off the corner to block the kick, and then turned downfield to block for the return. Our returner crossed the field to my side, and I picked out a player to lay the wood on. I dropped my shoulder and jumped right into his chest, making him do a back flip and land on his head. We scored on the play, while the guy I flattened was still on the ground. Next thing you know, I saw a Western coach taking his headphones off and running on the field to fight me. I couldn't believe it. I had never seen that before. Players and coaches had to hold him back. We won easily, 61-7.

Our next game was against Dillard High School. A lot of my family members went to Dillard, and I knew that a lot of great athletes came out of there, including Chris Gamble. The trash talking was at an all-time high, all the way down to our families. It seemed to get in our heads. When the game started, we were being called for penalties that we didn't usually get, like personal fouls, false starts, and offsides. But we got it together and pulled out a victory, 21-14. Now it was time for the playoffs.

In the first round, we beat Atlantic High School. Up next was against Blanche Ely High School. This was a huge game. All week we heard all the trash they were talking about us. So we started talking it back all the way up until game day. When we got off the bus and walked into their stadium, it was so packed that people had to watch the game from the railroad tracks. We were in Pompano, where my dad grew up. He had everybody and their grandma at the game supporting me.

Midway through the second quarter, Ely ran a dive play, and the running back bounced it to the outside. I ran downhill full speed and dropped my shoulder right into his chest. He fell backwards flat on his back and dropped the ball. The whole crowd went nuts. I went down just as hard with a shoulder stinger. But that set the tone for the day. We won, 21-19. This was the best Ely had ever played us, and I gave props where props were due.

In the third round, we faced Bradenton Manatee High School. In a hard-fought battle, we beat them, 45-17. We were back in the championship game. For the second year in a row, we would play Lakeland for the title. We were super-hyped to get revenge for our loss in 2004. They were ranked #1 and we were #2. Our offense was firing on all cylinders, and we were rocking on defense.

The game was right in our backyard, at the Miami Dolphins stadium. Early on, it looked like a blowout, by Lakeland. Once we started to get in our groove, it was too little, too late. In the fourth quarter, I got my ankle rolled up on and was in a lot of pain. But there was no way I was leaving this game. They ended up winning 39-10.

We were devastated afterward about the loss. I cried because I felt like this was supposed to be our year. Falling short hurt me bad. Still, we finished the season at 12-2, and I recorded 58 tackles and six interceptions. Despite another loss in the state championship, I had a feeling that something big was within my reach.

CHAPTER 4
SENIOR MOMENTS

Major, this is the best decision of your life.

Urban Meyer has been right about a lot of things in football ... and life. This was another instance. He said these words to me after I told him I wanted to play for Florida. It was a big relief when I finally made my decision.

After my junior season, it was as if Pandora's box had opened. I made All American and All County, and was named a 4-star player. Scholarship offers from all over started to pour in. I could have never imagined things going this way, with me moving so often and having to start over again and again. But at this point in my life, I wouldn't have asked for anything to be different.

During the off-season, I ran track again. I also got closer to Cris Carter and his family. I spent a bunch of weekends at his house, with his wife Melanie, his son Duron, who was a freshman, and his daughter, Monterae, who was in the 8th grade. Being away from my neighborhood was good for me. It helped me stay out of trouble. Another notable event happened when I cut my dreads off, which gave me more of a clean-cut, pretty-boy look going into my senior year.

I was now known around town as "Major Pain," because I always brought the pain on opponents. At the beginning of the school year, our communications class wanted me to do a TV show called "Major Pain." It would consist of me tackling students who were doing something they had no business doing. They said it would be played every Friday morning during announcements. Of course I said yes. It was so dope.

When the 2006 season began, Coach Carter wanted to switch it up and put a few plays in on offense for me. Most of it was me going in motion, and cracking the defensive end. We stormed through our first few opponents, putting up 31 points against Cypress Bay High School and 79 points against Cooper City High School. Through three games, we had allowed just 16 points. When we played Stoneman Douglas High School, we had to deal with their huge and impressive tight end. The first time I saw him, he seemed like he was twice my size. Before the game, he talked trash to me, telling me that I looked like a little kid and that I might want to put on my "big boy" pads. That got me so pumped up. *I'm gonna put him out the game for trying me like that.*

Early in the second quarter, I caught him coming across the middle, and dropped the boom on him. I lifted him off his feet, putting him flat on his back. I looked down and told him that my pads fitted just fine. He didn't return for the rest of the game. Stoneman Douglas went down just as easy, 45-7.

Things, meanwhile, were getting a little heated for me. Everyone wanted to know where I was headed to college. At the time, my family and I had no clue. In fact, I didn't really want to think about it during the season at all. I told everyone I would let them know when I was ready.

Through nine games, we were 8-1, our only loss coming to Deerfield High School, 18-15. After three more wins, we faced Ely again. They were stacked with talent, including guys like Patrick Peterson, JT Thomas, and Josh Moore, just to name a few. We still beat them, 45-8.

From there, we went to the playoffs, and won again in a blowout in the first round against Atlantic. In the second round, we faced Coconut Creek High School and shut them out too. At the same time, I was also focused on my future, talking to my family about colleges. Coach Smith wanted me to select my top five schools. After giving it some thought, I settled on Ohio State, Florida, Notre Dame, Miami, and USC.

Next up was Manatee High School. They came out swinging, and the next thing you know, it's tied 22-22 in the third quarter. Manatee had the ball deep in our territory with two minutes left. They motioned a receiver across the formation, bringing him to my side. On the snap, he ran a wheel route. I stayed with him, flipping my hips and turning my head to see if the ball was coming. It sure was, I intercepted the ball on the 4 yard line, took it all the way back across the field, jumping over my teammates that were blocking for me, made it to our 11 yard line getting pushed out of bounce. I was supper tired and could barely finish the game. We went on to win, 36-29, and advanced to the state championship and guess who was back there too? You got that right—Lakeland, our worst nightmare.

Since this was my senior year, I felt I had no choice but to come out of this game victorious. Then our offense goes out and fumbles on our 40 yard line on our first possession. It was my time to make a statement. On the very next play, I met the fullback head-on in the hole with a massive collision.

Still, we fell behind 7-0 after a 6-yard touchdown run by Chris Rainey. We got the ball back and drove to their 10-yard-line, but the drive was stopped short of a touchdown and our field goal was blocked. Moments later, Rainey scored a 73-yard touchdown, putting them up 14-0. Our teams then traded turnovers. We did nothing with ours, but they turned theirs into another touchdown. We were down 21-0 at the half.

I was so furious that I wanted to hurt one of their players. We opened the second half with the ball and turned it over again. I had had enough. When Lakeland ran a reverse to my side, I fought off a block, and hit the runner so hard that I put him to sleep on the field, literally. He got up and started walking to our sideline.

The game moved into the fourth quarter with the score was still 21-0. With 8:49 left, our fans started to leave the stadium, we finally got on the scoreboard with a touchdown. But Lakeland responded with another score to make it 28-7. That's when things really got interesting. We scored a 73-yard touchdown, and then Rainy answered right back with a 53-yarder of his own. We returned the kickoff to their 20-yard-line, and found the end zone on a fourth-down play. The score was now 35-21 with 1:48 remaining, and the fans started coming back.

We lined up for an onside kick, and I recovered it. Seconds later, we scored again to make it 35-28. Our fans were going nuts. We lined up for another onside kick. This time, my teammate Jeff Fuller, who played linebacker, recovered it. On the next play, we tied the game, sending it into overtime. I couldn't really believe what was happening.

Each team scored in the first overtime period. In the second, we held Lakeland to a field goal. Down 45-42, we were sure this game was ours. But on fourth and inches from the goal line, we ran a dive and were stopped short. It was the third time that Lakeland got the best of us. I was crushed.

The blow was taken easier when I looked back on my accomplishments in my senior season. I had 72 tackles and 3 interceptions. I was a finalist for the Hall Trophy, and was named the country's best defensive back by the U.S. Army. Now it was time to focus on the next step in my football career.

I started taking visits to schools all over the country. I went with my dad to Notre Dame. It was too cold and too quiet. Next was Ohio State. I had the time of my life there. At the end of my visit, Coach Jim Tressel sat me down in his office and asked what I was going to do. I told him I wanted to be a Buckeye, but didn't make a full commitment.

A week later, I visited Florida. I fell in love with everything they had going on—winning games and all the parties. Coach Meyer asked me the same question that Coach Tressel did. I told him I wanted to be a Gator. Coach Meyer was pleased, and told me that I made a great decision.

I did go on one last visit, to Miami. Honestly, I knew I wasn't going there because they weren't good at the time. So my choices narrowed to Ohio State, which had just lost the National Championship, and Florida, which had just won it. I talked to my family, and we thought long and hard on the decision before us. My mom even did a three-day fast and prayed on it to be sure I would make the right decision.

Florida had a lot of advantages over Ohio State. It was close to home, my family wouldn't have to spend tons of money to come see me play, and the weather was clearly to my liking. In addition, their best safety, Reggie Nelson, had just entered the NFL Draft. All this made it a much easier choice, and I officially committed to the Gators. With the other players who had also committed, I knew we were in great shape to win another National Championship.

CHAPTER 5
STARTING TIME

*Baby, I am proud of you. Keep up the great work
and continue to make me proud.*

There's nothing better than making your mom proud. I had done that by keeping my nose clean and turning myself into a blue chip prospect on the football field. Now, I was ready to take the next step in my career.

Signing Day arrived on February 7, 2007. We were so excited as a family. I walked into the St. Thomas cafeteria, where lots of friends and families were gathered. It was a great feeling knowing that all the hard work we put in as a team was about to pay off. When I sat down to make my announcement, I had three hats in front of me: Miami, Ohio State, and Florida. Then I told everyone in attendance that I had chosen the Gators. I got a great reaction from the crowd.

I thought for a moment about the rest of my teammates—17 guys got full rides, 10 of them were for D1 schools. I was the only one who committed to Florida. Coach Urban Meyer had put together an amazing recruiting class. In fact, it was ranked #1 in the country. I couldn't have been any happier.

I finished my senior year on a strong note and graduated St. Thomas with a 3.2 grade point average. I was super-excited about going to college, being on my own and doing what college students do. My mom had instilled greatness in me, and I felt big things were on the horizon. On the drive up to Gainesville, she cried tears of joy.

In college, you meet people from different walks of life, different ethnicities, and different religions. But you all have one thing in common: to become as successful as possible in your chosen field. College sometimes can be scary, being away from home and not around your blood family. But I had it so easy because my teammates welcomed me with open arms.

Being a part of the University of Florida football team made me hold myself to standards at a whole different level. Coach Meyer told us we had to be accountable, reliable, responsible, and train like a champion. The Gators had won the 2006 National Championship. That team's recruiting class had also been ranked #1. That was a lot to live up to. But our 2007 class was full of studs with dreams of winning another National Championship and playing at the next level.

I quickly found that being a part of something that is bigger than you forces you to want more for yourself. My goals were not just my goals. I had a team full of guys who were counting on me to do my part. This is what made me go extra hard. I never wanted to be that guy who let his teammates and family down.

Entering my freshman season, my mindset was to figure out my role on the team and do my part. I started on three of our four special teams: kickoff, punt, and punt return. My goal was to eventually become a starter on defense. In order to make that happen, I had to make my mark on special teams.

All freshmen playing for Coach Meyer had a stripe of black tape down the middle of their helmet. The only way you could get it off was by doing something to prove yourself to the team. I knew what I could bring to the team, but the only way for me to show it was with pads on. I would always tell myself that my coaches really didn't know what I was capable of. This motivated me to give them firsthand evidence.

We had our first day of practice in shoulder pads and helmets in August. I was focused and locked in on impressing my coaches and teammates. I barely spoke to anyone. When we started the team period—offense against defense—I took it upon myself to treat this like a live game situation. Jon Brently, a quarterback in my class, handed the ball off to Chris Rainey, the guy who used to run all over us in high school in the state championship games. I read the play and immediately started running the alley. Rainey stuck his foot into the ground and tried to cut back on me. But before he could do that, I rocked his world. All of my teammates circled around me, celebrating that hit, and Coach Meyer shut the rest of practice down.

In meetings later on that night, Coach Meyer called up Dorian Munroe. He was my "big brother" on the team. Every freshman had one assigned to him. When Dorian got to the front of the room, Coach Meyer told him to remove the black strip from my helmet. That was a proud moment. I was the first freshman to lose his black stripe. From that day forth, my teammates knew that I was all business.

We opened the 2007 season with 49-3 win at home against Western Kentucky. I ended up getting in on defense in the fourth quarter.

It was a great way to start my college career. My role on the team was limited at the time, but I knew the opportunity to do more would come. Kyle Jackson, the senior at safety, was in his first year as a starter, having sat behind Reggie Nelson. I was in line behind him.

In our next game, we faced Troy. They gave us all we could handle, but we pulled out a tough 59-31 victory. That set up a crucial game against our SEC rival Tennessee. We knew that we were going to have to bring it. With four minutes remaining in the first quarter, we ran a cowboy blitz on a third down play. That's when the cornerback blitzes and the safety covers his man on the outside. Tennessee reacted with a quick pass, but Kyle was late getting there and missed the tackle. Coach Meyer was furious. He looked around for me. *Major, get in there for Kyle.*

I sprinted onto the field, but Kyle waved me off. He wasn't coming out of the game, so I ran back to the sideline. On the next play, Kyle missed another tackle. Coach Meyer called a timeout, and asked me why I wasn't on the field. I told him that Kyle wouldn't leave the game. Coach Meyer was about to send security to escort him to the sideline, but our strong safety, Tony Joiner, talked some sense into him. We went on to win, 59-20, and I had become the starting safety. My dreams were beginning to come true. I wasn't going to look back.

In October, we played the Kentucky Wildcats. They had not beaten us in 20 years, but this would not be an easy game. Kentucky was 6-2 and ranked #7 in the country. At 5-2, we were #15. On their first possession, the Wildcats drove 78 yards and scored to go up 7-0. We responded with a pair of touchdowns to take the lead. In the second quarter, the Wildcats went for it on a fourth down at our 36-yard-line. Their tight end caught a pass over the middle for a first down, and I brought him down with a big hit. When I got up, I felt a stinging heat in my right thumb. I told Tony, and he said to ignore it. *Little nigga, you ain't getting out. You better play with it.*

Two plays later, Coach Meyer called a timeout. I jogged right over to the trainers. They said my thumb might be broken, and told Coach Meyer that I needed to take an X-ray. Unfortunately, it confirmed the bad news. We wound up beating Kentucky, 45-37, but my future was uncertain.

The next day, I was scheduled for surgery. One of our receivers, Riley Cooper, had also broken a finger in the Kentucky game, so he was in the same boat as me. I wanted my mom by my side, but she couldn't make it because of work. Luckily, Riley's dad and sister showed up, and gave me the emotional support I needed. I had a metal plate inserted in my thumb, with six screws to hold it down.

Right out of surgery, Riley and I had to get ready for our next game against Georgia. I was cleared to play, as long as my thumb was covered securely. Our training staff came up with this brilliant idea of putting a boxing glove on my right hand. I was skeptical at first, but I went out and played against Georgia. I wish my presence would have made a difference, but we lost, 42-30.

That was our third defeat in four games, putting us at 5-3. We responded with four straight wins, including a 45-12 massacre of Florida State. That helped us earn a spot in the Capital One Bowl against Michigan. They beat us, 41-35.

We ended the season at 9-4, but no one was happy. This was way below our expectations. Despite my broken thumb, I finished my freshman year with 67 tackles (47 solos) 4 forced fumbles and one interception. I was named an All American as well. But I had my sights set on bigger goals. I had already earned the starting safety job. Now, I wanted to win a National Championship.

CHAPTER 6

LIVING THE DREAM

I was about to play for a national championship, only 20 minutes away from my hometown. There was no better way to show out for my city.

Sometimes it's hard to believe that the life you're living is really yours. That's how I felt in January of 2009, as we were about to take the field at the Orange Bowl against Oklahoma for the National Championship. I had dreamed of a moment like this one. Now, it was actually happening.

Entering my sophomore year, I knew if I did not bust my behind getting better as a complete player, I could lose my starting job. Our off-season workout program was a beast, and got me in the best shape of my life. Waking up for 6am mat drills and pushing each other to their limit brought us all closer together as a team. Some players got choked out, others walked out, and fights were common. For every game we lost in 2007, the entire team had to run up and down the stairs around the whole stadium. It was really intense.

Our 2008 season opener came in late August against Hawaii. There was no better way for me to start the season than with a 56-10 victory and my first pick-6 as a Gator. Our crowd at the Swamp was so loud. When I scored, I celebrated with my teammates in the end zone. It was a great day.

Next up was Miami. This was a big game for me, because a lot of my family members were huge fans of the Hurricanes. But on this day they were in my corner. We beat Miami, 26-3, and then got ready for our next opponent, Tennessee. We handled them with ease to move our record to 3-0.

At this point, we were feeling really good about the way the season was going. But I honestly believe we became over-confident. We took our next game against Ole Miss for granted, which is something a team should never do. The mistake was costly. We lost to the Rebels, 31-30. One of the worse feelings as a team is getting outplayed by an opponent you know you're better than.

After the Ole Miss loss, Tim Tebow took the podium and made his famous promise speech, telling everyone that our team would not lose another game. We stood behind our quarterback 100%. His words fired all of us up. The following week, practice was very intense as we prepared to visit Arkansas. We knew that we could not overlook this team. We were dominant on both sides of the ball in a 38-7 win.

That set up a critical game against a big-time SEC rival, LSU. In 2008, they beat us in Baton Rouge, 28-24. We knew they were going to put up a fight in the Swamp. We saw this as a perfect opportunity to show the world that we were not to be messed with. We attacked this game like it was for a championship and went on to beat them, 51-21.

We followed that with another laugher, beating Kentucky 63-5. At this point, everything was back on track. Our offense was unstoppable, our defense was making plays every time it had to, and our special teams were giving us the best field position possible. On November 1, we faced Georgia in a game that was very personal for all of us. When they beat us the year before, we felt totally disrespected. After their first touchdown, their bench cleared, and every single player, coach, and trainer ran to the end zone to celebrate. As we saw it, this was one of the most embarrassing moments in college football history. If we could put up 100 points and break the scoreboard, that's exactly what we were going to do.

There was so much tension before this game even kicked off. Our middle linebacker, Brandon Spikes, told us he would bust Georgia running back Knowshon Moreno right in his mouth. Brandon was a man of his word, so I knew this wasn't just talk.

We won the coin toss and deferred to the second half. On Georgia's very first snap, the ball went to Moreno, and Brandon put him on his back to set the tone for the rest of the game. Our defense never let up. We picked off three passes, and Ahmad Black had a 64 yards return interception putting us into the Bulldogs' redzone. The final score was 49-10. What a statement game!

We continued that momentum in our next three games, victories over Vanderbilt, South Carolina, and the Citadel. Our final game of the regular season came against Florida State. Things got really heated during warm-ups when Ahmad began taunting an FSU player. Both teams were ready to go at it. Our coaches had to come between all of us to break it up. They wanted us to focus on the task at hand. *Allow your play to speak for you.*

We ended up doing just that. From the opening kickoff through the final whistle, we handed them an ass whipping they had never experienced. Even a driving rainstorm couldn't stop us. Percy Harvin got us on the scoreboard first, and they responded with a field goal to make it 7-3. On FSU's next possession, I intercepted a pass, which gave us good field position. With the weather getting uglier, we were forced to keep the ball on the ground and limit the passing. Our offense didn't miss a beat. We took a 21-9 halftime lead, but that wasn't good enough for us. We punished them in the second half and won 45-15. It was our fifth straight victory over FSU and the seventh game in a row that our offense scored at least 42 points.

After beating FSU we were preparing for Alabama, the #1 team in the country, in the SEC Championship in Atlanta. We were right behind them at #2 in the rankings. Coach Meyer told us this was going to be a physical, smash-mouth game. We couldn't wait. Our only concern was the loss of Percy. He hurt his leg against FSU and was ruled out.

When game day arrived, it finally hit me how fortunate we were to be playing for the conference title. Not many teams or players make it this far. I was determined to capitalize on this opportunity. We received the opening kickoff, and marched down for a touchdown. Alabama responded just as quickly to tie the game at 7-7. Minutes later, they kicked a field goal to go ahead. This was the first time we had been down since our loss to Ole Miss, but we didn't panic.

It was time for the defense to step up. Alabama drove into our territory and lined up for a field goal attempt. Only they faked it. Terron Sanders, aka Sandy Man, wasn't fooled and made a hell of a play to stop them. That gave us momentum. We tied the game a short time later, and then Tebow connected with David Nelson for a 5-yard touchdown pass. We were up 17-10 going into halftime.

The mood in our locker room was really intense and emotional. We knew that we weren't playing up to our full potential. Our coaches felt they could be better, too. As a team, we decided to take it to another level. But Alabama was fired up as well. They opened the third quarter with a 91-yard scoring drive to tie the score. Then they got the ball back and kicked a field goal, putting them up 20-17.

No one on our sideline ever lost faith. From that point on, we seized control and cruised to a 31-20 victory. We were SEC champs! It was the best feeling ever. We partied hard in Atlanta, but also knew that we had unfinished business. We got the news that we were playing Oklahoma for the National Championship, in Miami.

We had almost a full month to prepare for the Sooners. They had the #1 offense in the country, so we took the opportunity to get healthy and learn as much as we could about them. For me, playing for the National Championship just 20 minutes from where I grew up was a dream come true. There was no better way to prove to my family and friends what I was made of. I felt that I had to play the best game of my life.

Game day finally arrived on January 8, 2009. I had so many emotions running through me. They were almost uncontrollable. I remembered the prayer my mother always told me. *I can do all things through Christ who strengthens me.*

During warm-ups, I kept repeating that prayer. When it was time for all the defensive backs to come together, I looked each and every one in the eyes and told them that I was laying it all on the line tonight. No matter what, I would have their backs.

Oklahoma received the opening kickoff, and immediately went into an up-tempo, no-huddle offense. The game speed caught us a little by surprise, and by second down we were a bit winded. On the next play, Oklahoma quarterback Sam Bradford pump faked to my right side as his receiver, Manny Johnson, ran a double move on Joe Haden. I read the play, and saw Joe was behind a step. Bradford let the pass go, I broke on the ball but I had no interest in an interception. I wanted to let the Sooners—and the world—know that I was going to give them hell for all four quarters. I delivered a killer shot on our sideline that separated Johnson from the ball and put him on the bench to recover. Just like I said before the game, I had Joe's back.

After a scoreless first quarter, Tebow put us ahead with a 20-yard touchdown pass to Louis Murphy. Oklahoma then got into gear, and tied the game with a quick scoring drive. On their next possession, they marched down to our goal line. The Sooners went for it on fourth down, but Torrey Davis made an amazing stop to give the ball back to our offense. Minutes later, they got the ball back and drove all the way to our 3-yard line. This time the secondary stepped up. A pass by Bradford was tipped by three guys before it ended up in my hands. This was our 25th interception of the season, which set a new school record. We went into the half tied 7-7.

As I looked around the locker room, I knew we hadn't played our best. The feeling was shared by my teammates and coaches. We all locked arms, looked each other in the eyes, and promised to give our maximum effort for the next 30 minutes.

On our second possession of the third quarter, Tebow led the offense on an amazing drive capped by a touchdown from Percy, making the score 14-7. We felt we were now in our groove, but Oklahoma responded with a scoring drive of its own. The game was tied again.

Minutes later, we kicked a field goal to retake the lead. Then Ahmad came up with our 2nd interception of the game. With the ball in the air, I made a beeline for the receiver and delivered another big hit. I knocked the crap out of Ahmad at the same time, but he managed to hold on to the pass for his seventh interception of the season. It was one of the greatest picks I have ever witnessed. Tebow converted the turnover into a touchdown, and we never looked back. The final score was 24-14. We were national champions!

There was no better feeling. At every level in every sport, your goal is to win a championship. I had done it at the ultimate stage of college, in front of people who had known me my entire life. Later that evening, we went out to Dream Nightclub in Miami Beach, I danced all night and had the time of my life.

CHAPTER 7

THREE'S A CROWD

How do you want to be remembered?

That question kept running through my mind after the 2008 season. Over the past 12 months, I had learned a lot about what it takes to achieve your goals. We could have given up after our loss to Ole Miss. But if we had, we would not have won the National Championship. I took away two key points. 1. As a team, there is nothing you cannot accomplish when working together. 2. Never lose focus on your goals.

As a player, I had come a long way. I started in all 14 games in 2008, recording 66 tackles (including 30 solos), four interceptions (including my first pick-6), two forced fumbles, and five pass break-ups.

We kicked off the 2009 season ranked #1 in the preseason polls. Charleston Southern visited the Swamp for our opener. Our mindset was to start fast every game, and that's exactly what we did against the Buccaneers in a 62-3 blowout. I contributed with my first interception of the year. We did much the same in our next game, a 56-6 win over Troy. Janoris Jenkins picked off a pass, marking our 14th straight game with an interception.

A week later, Tennessee visited the Swamp. Even though they had not beaten us in the last four years, we weren't going to take them lightly. Coach Meyer made sure special teams, defense, and offense were all on the same page. We were up 13-6 at the half, but our coaches blasted us in the locker room for playing down to our opponent. Joe Haden intercepted a pass to start the third quarter, and our offense converted it into a field goal. Ahmad Black added another interception later on, and we held on for a 23-13 victory. At 3-0, we were feeling good about ourselves.

Things changed for me the following week. In fact, my whole college world was shaken up and would never be the same. As we prepared for Kentucky, the coaches made a move that I don't understand to this day. They inserted freshman Will Hill into the safety picture, and created a three-man rotation. I brushed it off at first, thinking that maybe the coaches were trying to give me and Ahmad a little more rest. But on game day our position coach Chuck Heater told us that we would keep the rotation. Ahmad and I looked at each other. We were confused and at a loss for words. Staying quiet was unusual for me. I was seriously mad, but I didn't want this to affect my play.

Unfortunately, the rotation only became more frustrating and annoying. For the first time in my career, I began to understand how a coach could let you down. I thought back to when Coach Meyer recruited me. I remembered him sitting in our home talking to my family. My mother and I trusted him completely. He was a big part of my decision to commit to Florida. He made me feel like I was a part of his family. Now, I felt betrayed. This was not how you treated family.

As an athlete, you constantly face challenges on and off the field. I felt like I was being tested. I reminded myself that while I could not control this situation, I could control the plays that I made. Despite my diminished role, I played well against Kentucky. We beat them 41-7, and I picked off another pass. I thought about meeting with the coaches after the game, but Ahmad talked with them and passed on their promise that they would "fix it."

As we started preparing for our next game, against LSU, there was a lot of tension between players and coaches. I tried to keep a positive attitude, but I really did not understand what was going on. Not wanting to be a distraction to the whole team, I focused on my job and had a great week of practice. Things seemed to be back to normal, so I was feeling a little better.

A game in Baton Rouge is always an adventure. As we pulled up to the stadium that Saturday, their fans began throwing things at our bus. Coach Meyer got hit by a beer in the leg, and was fuming about it. In the locker room, he gathered us together. *Look at how their fans treat us. They are very disrespectful. If you are not ready to play by now, you can stay in the locker room.*

Man, after that speech, the team was so crunk. As we ran out onto the field for warm-ups, we couldn't help but see this huge roaring tiger in a cage right outside of our locker room. You couldn't avoid being a little afraid. I had never been that close to a tiger in my life. I won't lie. It scared me.

The game was a defensive struggle from the first snap. The LSU crowd was going crazy. I was sitting right next to Joe on the bench, yelling his name to get his attention. But the fans were so loud that he could not hear me. Finally, I tapped him on the shoulder and screamed that this was one of the loudest stadiums that we had ever played in. He agreed. But the noise had little effect on us. We won 13-3 and moved to 5-0.

Up next was Arkansas. Coach Meyer warned us not to take them lightly. During practice that week, we went back to the three-man rotation at safety. I damn sure felt some type of way about this, and it seemed to impact the entire team. Game day had arrived, and our usual energy wasn't there. After a scoreless first quarter, Arkansas went ahead 7-0. Then we traded field goals, making the score 10-3 going into halftime.

The second half went back and forth. We were tied in the fourth quarter when the Razorbacks put together an 87-yard touchdown drive that put them up 20-13. Our offense answered right back with a touchdown by Jeff Demps. With time running down, Arkansas moved into field goal range but missed the kick. We got the ball back on our 20-yard-line, marched down the field and put the game away with a field goal. Our undefeated season continued.

Still, after this game, it was real hard for me to hide my emotions. My family noticed my limited playing time and wondered if I had gotten hurt. I told them I was healthy. The problem was the three-man rotation. We agreed that we should get to the bottom of the issue, and tried to schedule a meeting with Coach Meyer. But he told me to talk to our defensive coordinator, who then told me to talk to Coach Heater. He said I was playing great football, but the decision was over his head. I left that meeting feeling unsure and unsatisfied. But I told myself that this was a teachable moment. I refused to place myself before my team.

My family was far more upset. They wanted to talk to the coaches personally, but I told them to let me handle it. I had a conversation with Cris Carter, and asked for his advice. *When you are on that field, make sure that everyone knows you are out there. Even if you are only playing 10 snaps per game, make all 10 count.*

Our next opponent was a very talented Mississippi State team. It was a hard-fought game that featured plenty of big defensive plays, including my third interception of the year. We won 29-19, and improved to 7-0. The rotation was still in place, and I tried to stay calm about it.

On Halloween, we met Georgia in another heated matchup. Our defense dominated, picking off four passes in a 41-17 victory. It was bittersweet for me. I was really getting fed up with the way things were going. After the game, I vented once again to my family. I didn't know what to do at this point. Joe and I had a long conversation late into the night. *Maj, they are not doing you right. Bro, if you decided to leave and you don't get drafted and nothing happens for you, I gotcha.*

Those words meant a lot to me. I shed a few tears because I felt like that was the push I needed. The next day, my mother and I scheduled a meeting with the coaching staff. I started talking as soon as we sat down, and got everything off my chest. Coach Meyer saw how upset I was and said that things would go back to normal. I didn't know if I could believe him. We weren't just talking about my Florida career. This had to do with my future in the NFL. If teams didn't see me as a starter, my status in the draft could be affected. Coach Meyer assured me that the situation would be fixed. But my head was spinning. After that meeting, my mother and I went home and prayed. We asked God to lead my life and pick what's right for me.

Leaving everything in God's hands took stress off me. We hosted Vanderbilt the following week, and blew them out, 27-3. The 9-0 start was just the third time happening in school history. It felt amazing to be a part of something special. Next, we traveled to South Carolina to play the Gamecocks. Joe had a remarkable game with one pick, a sack, 11 tackles, two forced fumbles, and one pass break-up. He showed why he was the #1 corner in college football. With our 24-14 victory, our winning streak spanning back to 2008 extended to 20 games in a row, a new school record.

We moved it to 21 straight with a win over Florida International University. That set up our annual game against FSU. This was very important to me, as it was potentially my last home game. That's because I was now considering declaring myself eligible for the NFL Draft. I flashed back to a memorable moment against the Seminoles when Aaron Hernandez caught a pass, shook FSU's entire defense and scored a touchdown. He threw the ball in the stands, walked to the sidelines and told Coach Meyer he was entering the draft. That had always stuck with me.

FSU was no match for us. We rolled to a 37-10 win, and in turn became the first Florida team to post a 12-0 regular season record. I remembered coming in as part of the 2007 class and saying that we wanted to make history. Mission accomplished.

Going into the SEC Championship against Alabama, we had our hands full. They were 12-0 as well, and ranked #2 in the country. We knew exactly what they wanted to do: pound the football and make us stop them. On this day, Alabama was too much for us to handle. They ended our winning streak with a 32-13 whipping.

Right after the game, it was time to sit down with my family and discuss my future as a Gator. It was an emotional conversation. My mom was afraid that if I returned to Florida, I would be back in an uncertain situation that would only hurt my draft status further.

She wanted me to get my degree, but not at the expense of my pro career. *Don't leave your future in their hands.*

I agreed. I felt I had accomplished everything I wanted to at Florida. I had matured as a player and a person. My legacy was cemented. Plus, the coaches had forced my hand. I told my mother I would declare for the NFL Draft. I would make my announcement after the Sugar Bowl.

CHAPTER 8

THE NEED FOR SPEED

*I have to be better than yesterday, and if yesterday was great,
I will make today amazing.*

When you decide to make the NFL your career, you have to take a good, hard look at the player you really are. There's no room for anything less than your absolute best. Once I was certain I was leaving school, I knew it was time to grow up. My future depended on it.

As we started to prepare for the Sugar Bowl against Cincinnati, Ahmad Black asked me if I was coming back for my senior season. I told him I was out of here. He thought I was kidding around. I could see where he was coming from. I had never really considered an early exit from Florida until the stuff with the three-man rotation started. My decision would be a surprise to just about everyone.

The Sugar Bowl was now even more special to me and my family. This was the first game I really could embrace and enjoy, knowing it was my last time putting on the Gator uniform and playing with my brothers. At the same time, part of me felt like I was being rushed out.

Leading up to the game, all we kept hearing about was the high-powered Cincinnati offense. While we were in New Orleans, we bumped into some of their players, and they started selling out to us like we were a pushover team. We weren't having any of it. *Mark our words. We'll make you all eat them words.*

That's just what we did. Cincinnati didn't stand a chance against us. We beat them, 51-24. After the game, it got emotional for me knowing I wasn't coming back. The next day would be my final meeting with the coaches. At the time, they knew nothing about my decision.

That evening felt like the night before the first day of school. I couldn't sleep for nothing because I was trying to prepare my speech. But the next day as I waited for my turn to see the coaches, my mind went blank and I forgot everything. As I walked in the room, I started to shed a few tears. I looked at my coaches and told them that they had done me and my family wrong this past season. We believed it was best that I entered the NFL Draft. They asked if there was anything they could do to change my mind. I told them no and wished them the best in the upcoming season. They wished me well in the draft. It felt like a whole weight was lifted off of me.

Next, I had a one-on-one meeting with my cornerback coach, Vance Bedford. He grabbed an old playbook from the Chicago Bears, the team he used to coach for. *Major, this is how big an NFL playbook is. You'll have to learn it inside and out. You're going to do great. Good luck.*

I finished my college career with 165 total tackles, eight interceptions, five forced fumbles, and 15 pass break-ups—all this in just three years. I had also learned three important lessons. 1. Take advantage of every opportunity. 2. Keep your composure. 3. Be strong through whatever you're facing.

My next big step was finding an agent, as well as a place to continue working out. This was a difficult choice to make. Having the right representation speaks volumes to NFL teams. And working with a trainer who knows how to make your speed and strength numbers improve is just as crucial. This was especially true for me, since I didn't know where I would fall at in the draft.

I ended up going with XPE Sports out of Boca Raton. The head guy there was Tony Villani. He was known for dramatically raising the numbers for draft prospects. As for my agent, I went with a friend of the family, Mitch Frankel of Impact Sports. When I met with him, the first thing we needed to do was call the NFL to see what round I was projected to go. Already, things were feeling intense. *Mr. Wright, we have you projected to go no later than the 3rd round.*

That information gave me ammo to work really hard. Meanwhile, my agent did his homework on what the scouts were saying about my weaknesses. The main one was my speed—they didn't think I was fast enough. I ran this by Tony. He promised to get me down to a 4.4 in the 40-yard dash. I have to admit that I was skeptical.

Being at a top facility like XPE was a big advantage. For instance, I was training with Eric Berry, the #1 projected safety in the 2010 draft class. So that right there was another reason for me to even go harder. On the first day we did testing, I saw my numbers and almost cried. My 40 time was 4.85. Tony told me not to worry. *Major, that's where I come in. I'll fix your technique, work on your explosion, and get you to hold your top-end speed.*

At this point I was working out every day with an eye on the NFL Combine. I had not been invited yet, but I was pretty sure I would be. I was studying like a mad man, learning offensive formations and knowing where the safeties and the linebackers dropped in zone defenses. This was important for the Combine. The coaches were known to ask players to get on the whiteboard to see how well they knew their defenses. Every morning after I woke up, I told myself that I would be better than the day before. I trained my mind so I would be ready for anything.

In January, my agent called to confirm that I had been invited to the Combine. That simply added more fuel to the fire. I got even more geeked after my second testing period. My 40 time dropped to 4.66! Soon I began to notice new confidence in my work ethic. There was no better reward than seeing my times fall. The hard work was really paying off.

Then I encountered a new challenge. Two weeks out from the Combine, my right knee started bothering me, especially when I got down in my running stance. Tony told me to get an MRI. I was instantly terrified. I prayed hard for it to be something minor. The results came back and showed I had a slight tear in my meniscus. I had a meeting with Tony and my agent. They asked whether I could get through the Combine. I told them I didn't really have a choice. This was an opportunity that comes once in a lifetime. I had to take care of my family.

The next few days had me a little shook. Every time I felt pain in my knee, I wondered if I was doing even more damage to it. My final testing was coming up, and I turned to God for help. I asked him to protect me from anything that would distract me from giving my very best. I approached my 40 with a clear mind and not once did I think about my knee. When it was my time to run, I took a deep breath and let it all out. I clocked a 4.52! Man, I was speechless. The rest of the drills felt like I was floating when I was doing them. I gave God all the praise for clearing my mind. I then called my agent and told him my time in the 40. At the time, I was the 10th safety on the board. If I could get my 40 time down to 4.4, I would likely go in the second round.

When it was finally time for the Combine, I was so excited. I spent the entire flight to Indianapolis studying and getting ready for the interview of my life. The night before, I couldn't sleep. The day started bright and early with a drug test at 5:30am. The next thing was seeing the doctors. I was a little scared that they would find the tear in my right knee, but I made it through because they only did X-rays. After that, I had meetings with two teams lined up: the Atlanta Falcons and Baltimore Ravens. It was a long day.

That night, I couldn't stop thinking about the opportunity that God had given me. I was about to kick in the front door of my childhood dreams. When it was time to get up, I said one last prayer and put my game face on.

The day began with my height and weight: 5-11 and 206lbs. Then I warmed up for the bench-press with Josh Moore, a defensive back from Kansas University, who also went to Ely High School in my hometown. We did five reps at 135lbs, three at 185lbs. and then two at 225lbs (the weight they tested at). Josh was first up to test, and I cheered him on. When the bar hit his chest on his first rep, he couldn't push it back up. He had wasted all energy warming up. That, of course, made me start questioning myself. As I got up under the bar, I was super-hyped. I knocked off a dozen reps with no problem, #13 was a struggle, and #14 was all I could handle before my arms felt like noodles. Man, I felt so good!

Next, was the vertical jump, which was never my best station. But I ended up hitting 37.5 inches, which felt great. From there, I went straight to the broad jump station. My goal was at least 10 feet. I came up just short at 9-11. The next two stations were the shuttle drill and the 3 cone drill. I came in at 4.3 seconds in the first one, and 6.9 seconds in the second one. So far, I was pleased with my results. I still had two very important stations left: the 40-yard dash and position drills.

I knew all the scouts thought I couldn't run on the next level, so the 40 was something I took to the heart. As I approached the starting line, I got down on my knee to take my stance. Then I began praying silently. *I can do all things through Christ who strengthens me.*

When I took off, everything felt so smooth. It was like I was flying. As soon as I crossed the finish line, I went right to get my phone to text my family. They texted me back saying that I had clocked a 4.48. That was unbelievable, and even better I still had a lot left in the tank. I thanked God and prepared for my next attempt. This time was even faster, a 4.44. I texted my family. *We did it!*

Well, almost. I still had to do my position drills. These take focus, discipline, and courage. Focus because you are live on TV, working out in front of your potential boss. Discipline for understanding your assignments and executing them. Courage for keeping your confidence, even if you mess up. I performed as well as I could have, and left Indianapolis with no regrets. In no time, I went from the 10th safety in the draft to the top five.

I returned to Boca to get ready for my Pro Day in March. I talked with my agent and trainer, and we decided it would be best for me to do board work and position drills only. Then I headed to

Gainesville, where I would meet with the Chicago Bears. I was the only safety working out for them, and I'm not lying when I tell you this workout was by far the most intense I have ever experienced. I first sat down with Jon Hoke, the defensive back coach for the Bears, and he went over the drills I would do. He asked the trainers to keep water close, which made me wonder what the hell I was getting myself into now! Still I was filled with confidence knowing I was going to kill this workout.

We started with all sorts of back-pedaling drills, left and right. I had to break down at 45 degrees and 90 degrees, and then catch the ball coming out of my break. I had to flip 180 degrees out of a back-pedal on the coach's command as well. There was also a sideline-to-sideline drill, with a full-out sprint after catching the ball. My heart was racing, and Coach Hoke asked if I needed a break. I told him no, and he started laughing.

After a brief rest, we started again. That's when I got my second wind. Coach Hoke wanted to simulate game-speed breaks using cover 2 and single high looks. In cover 2, both safeties line up 15 yards deep and three yards wide from the end man on the offensive line. In single high, only one safety is deep, 15 to 20 yards in the middle of the offensive formation. We did about 10 more drills, and I was dog-tired afterward. I joked with Coach Hoke that he was trying to break me. He told me that I was a tough cookie.

Next, we went to the classroom for board work. Coach Hoke handed me a black marker and a blue one, and told me to draw a 21 personnel with a pro formation. Then he wanted to see a base defense. When he asked me to draw an over front and an under front, I paused and stalled for time. Finally, I admitted that I didn't know either. He commended me for being honest. Most guys would have just made something up.

Despite that positive reinforcement, I left the meeting a little confused and a little down. I felt I had made a good showing, but there were still so many unknowns. I decided that all I could do was continue my preparation for the draft. Being in shape and mentally sharp were now my two primary goals.

CHAPTER 9
BEAR NECESSITIES

You are now a Chicago Bear. Be ready to work.

When I heard those words from Chicago head Coach Lovie Smith, I knew my life had changed forever. Football was no longer just my passion. It was a full-time job. I couldn't wait to start my career.

As the 2010 NFL Draft approached, it became clear that I wasn't going to be selected in the first round. That wasn't the case with my best friend Joe Haden. He was viewed as a top 10 pick, and that's exactly where he went. The Cleveland Browns took him with the seventh pick overall. I texted him with my congratulations, and then got ready for what could be a long wait.

The second day of the draft couldn't get here fast enough. My family and I loaded up at my Auntie Betty's house to watch. Two safeties had gone in the first round, which was expected. Two more went early in the second round, at #37 to the Philadelphia Eagles and #38 to Cleveland. When the San Francisco 49ers grabbed another safety with the 49th pick, I looked at my agent. *Are you sure you haven't missed a call or a text on your phone?*

When the second round ended and I hadn't been drafted, I was deep in my feelings. The Detroit Lions picked a safety at #66. I had never even heard of the guy. Five picks later, the Green Bay Packers selected another safety. *Are you kidding me? How was I still on the board?*

As I was taking all this in, my agent got a call from a number with a 708 area code. It was the Bears. My agent handed me the phone, and I ran outside. A lady on the other end asked if I was Major Wright. She told me to wait for Coach Smith and then put me on hold. He welcomed me to the team, and I thanked him for the opportunity.

I was officially the 75th pick in the draft. I laid down in the middle of the road and cried like a baby. When I went back in the house, I started celebrating with my family. My auntie Betty always kept her house real neat, someone popped a bottle of champagne and sprayed it all over. She was so mad, but I promised to pay whatever it cost to clean up the mess.

Looking back, I realized God had been throwing me signs all along that I would end up in Chicago. My coach at Florida had showed me a Bears playbook. The rental car I was driving had a Chicago license plate. The feeling of being drafted was unreal. Every kid who plays football dreams of making it to the NFL. Now it was really happening.

With rookie camp coming up soon, it was time to reset my mind back to attack mode. I had to prove to my new coaches that I was worth the draft pick. At the time, the Bears had two pretty good safeties, Chris Harris and Daniel Manning. Nothing would be handed to me. If I wanted to be a starter, I would have to earn it on the field.

The first step, however, was to sign my contract. My agent got me a four-year deal worth $2,634,700, with a signing bonus of $679,300. My rookie base salary was $315,000. It would rise to $605,000 in my second year and then to $609,000 in my third year. With escalators negotiated by my agent, I could make up to $1,323,000 in the last year of my contact. The money motivated me for sure.

Rookie camp started in late April. The first day consisted of one meeting after another. We learned how the Bears did things, their expectations of rookies, and the defenses we would install. There were drafted and undrafted guys from every college you can think of. I went in with an open mind, wanting to retain as much information as possible. I asked as many questions as I could. I didn't want my coaches to question my effort.

The next day was even more intense. Coach John Hoke gave us homework, and told us he would know who was studying and who wasn't. Did they have cameras in our rooms? I wasn't interested in finding out, so I worked my ass off. I went to sleep early that night knowing I had a long day ahead of me. I woke up the next morning before my alarm clock sounded.

Our first meeting that day was special teams. The coaches got me super-excited. Guys on special teams looked like they had so much fun. And blocking for the best returner in the game, Devin Hester, was an amazing opportunity.

Our next meeting was defense. For the first time, I sat down with Rod Marinelli, our defensive coordinator. He seemed like a straightforward dude. What stuck out to me was how he didn't want to hear how good you were. Rather, he wanted to see it on tape. We then moved to position meetings. The first thing Coach Hoke did was getting us on the board to see how much of the homework we retained. *How did I know I would be first up?*

I felt totally prepared, until I got to the front of the room. My confidence dropped as I picked up a black marker and a blue marker. Coach Hoke asked me to draw deuce personnel for the offense and an under-10 formation for the defense. Now, let me explain that all defenses are similar. What makes things difficult is the terminology each team uses. For example, deuce means one running back and two tight ends, while under-10 is a man-to-man defense where the Sam linebacker takes the tight end to the close call side and the free safety takes the other tight end.

Though I knew the defense he called, my mind went blank. As long as I was sitting down, I was good, but there was something about that walk up to the board and the markers that made me nervous. I did the best I could do, but Coach Hoke told me to sit down and had another player fix my mistakes. It made me feel a little better when all the other rookies screwed up, too.

After our meetings, it was time for lunch and then practice. I grabbed a snack and went downstairs to the locker room to study before heading out to the field. I felt like the Bears held me to a higher standard. I knew there was pressure on me. With that in mind, I decided to be the first to go in anything we did. Every drill felt like Coach Hoke critiqued me to the fullest. And I loved every bit of it. It was like my Pro Day all over again.

After position drills, it was one-on-ones, safeties versus tight ends and running backs. I was a little nervous because I knew that man coverage wasn't my strong point. First up was a tight end. He was 6-3 and at least 230lbs, with a little speed. None of that mattered. I was all over him and forced an incomplete pass. I was crunk! Next, I went against a running back, and he beat me. I asked to go one more time, and shut down another tight end.

Up next was the 7-on-7 period. There were a few plays where I could have put some of my teammates in the hospital, but it wasn't full contact. One thing that I had to get used to was picking up loose balls and running them back to the line of scrimmage. There were a few times I just forgot all about it and started walking off the field. Coach Hoke chewed me out every time I did that. In the offense vs. defense session, things got a little out of hand because everyone was trying so hard to impress the coaches. I was exhausted by the end of the day. When I got back to my hotel room, I studied for a while and fell asleep.

On the second day, my mindset was to avoid the mistakes I made the day before and ask more questions about how I could improve. Practice went much better, and I began to establish myself as a vocal leader. At the end of the day, I hung out with my fellow rookies at the hotel. We all knew of each other in college, but few of us had ever met in person. It was dope hearing about some of their college experiences.

The third day was the last day of rookie camp. I wanted to finish strong and leave my coaches with a great impression. I did that with a pick and a forced fumble in the team session. I was excited about my future.

That excitement sustained me as I prepared for OTAs (organized team activities). I was super-geeked to meet the rest of my teammates, guys I grew up watching like Brian Urlacher, Julius Peppers, and Charles Tillman. It was hard when I learned that some of the guys I knew from rookie camp had been cut, but I quickly learned that this was business in the NFL. I also learned a lot from Chris Harris. He took me under his wing and helped me get a full grasp on our defense. More than anything else, OTAs taught me how to be a pro.

When I returned home, I took a little time to relax and celebrate. Then it was back working my butt off. Training camp opened on July 30. It would be like walking blindfolded into the middle of nowhere. I wanted to be as prepared as possible.

A typical day in training camp alternates between meetings and practice. The Bears had me running with the second team defense and playing every special team. Morning practice on the first day was intense, long, hard and in hot, steamy conditions. During the break afterward, the vets ate a quick lunch and then headed to their rooms for a nap before our afternoon meetings. It took me a while to learn this lesson. While we were in our position meeting later that day, I started feeling super-tired. The next thing I knew, I was getting yelled at by a coach. *Major, I don't know what you did in college, but we don't sleep here. Next time I will fine you.*

After that, it was back on the field for our second practice of the day. It wasn't as intense as the morning session, but I was exhausted nonetheless. And the day still wasn't over, because we had more meetings. I got back to my room at 10pm. I was suddenly full of energy. I spent some time with some of the vets, and stayed up until about 1am. As the days passed, I started to adjust to my new schedule.

Our first preseason game came in mid-August against San Diego Chargers. The vets wouldn't be playing much, so I was set to see a lot of action, at least three quarters on defense, plus special teams. Chris Harris told me *Don't ask for a breather, rook.*

The night before, I couldn't sleep for nothing. Obviously, I was super-excited for my first game. But one of my really good friends, Rich Goodman, was playing for the Chargers. This was beyond a dream come true. We won the coin toss and deferred the ball to the second half. That meant defense was up first. I didn't have to wait long for my moment to shine. On the very first play, Ryan Mathews, San Diego's top pick in 2010, broke free in the open field and made it to my level. I lined him up and slammed him onto the turf. What an eye opener! But my night ended early when I broke my left index finger. In my first game as a Bear, I recorded 7 tackles and 25 snaps. I felt damn good about my performance and so did everyone else, although we lost 25-10. I had surgery a few days later. The injury sidelined me for the rest of preseason. It really sucked because at this point I was fighting for a starting job.

I tried to keep my head up and focus on my recovery. But as a rookie in the NFL, life can be tough when you're not on the field. Vets don't like it when you're hurt. One day I was in the training room talking to Devin Hester. Our center, Olin Kreutz, walked in and told me to shut my mouth. Olin had been in the league for 12 years, and no one ever messed with him. I didn't like how he treated me, but one of my teammates told me a story about one of the defensive lineman who got into it with Olin and he knocked him out cold in the weight room. From then on, I simply stayed away from him. All I could do was keep in shape and get ready for the season opener against the Detroit Lions.

CHAPTER 10
LESSONS LEARNED

*Only if I would have listened to my mom
and not acted like a Mr. Know It All.*

As a rookie in the NFL, you learn something new just about every day. You can't avoid it. You're constantly faced with situations you've never encountered before, on and off the field. Keeping your head above water can be a struggle. It really helps to rely on the people you know you can trust.

As we approached our first game of the 2010 season—the first of my NFL career—my finger was no longer an issue. But I still had to play with a splint on it. That whole week in practice, I was rotating in and out on defense, and starting on kickoff and punt. The night before our opener against the Detroit Lions, I didn't get any rest.

The atmosphere on game day was way different from the preseason. All the hype that I was hearing about was there. During the coin toss, I took the time to say a prayer, asking God to cover me while I gave it my all. Detroit wanted the ball, so defense was up first. I took the field with the kickoff team. Robbie Gould booted a touchback, so all I did was sprint down the field. I wound up playing 15 snaps on defense and made three tackles. We beat the Lions, 19-14. It was a great way to start my rookie season.

The following week, we traveled to Dallas to play the Cowboys. I couldn't wait to see their stadium. I had heard a lot about it. To get ready for the Cowboys, I spent time watching film with Coach Gill Byrd, trying to learn more about our system and get comfortable in it. I was still hesitant about things, and there is no room for any hesitation in the NFL. The more I learned, the faster I could play.

On Sunday morning, I brushed my teeth, washed my face and headed down to grab breakfast with my teammates. After going to chapel, I returned to my room, packed up and then got on the bus to head to the stadium. From the outside, I wasn't that impressed with the Cowboys' home. But once we were inside, I realized this was the best stadium I had ever seen. I mean, it had the biggest jumbotron scoreboard in the whole world hanging from the ceiling. The visitor locker room looked like the home locker room.

When I stepped on the field to warm up, things felt a little different. My legs were so stiff that I needed the trainer to help me stretch. We won the coin toss and deferred to the second half. I was so pumped, and the atmosphere in the stadium was nuts. But on the kickoff, I felt that same tightness, only worse than before. I went to the sideline, grabbed a black ball and rolled my hamstrings out.

A few minutes later, it was time for the punt team, and I was right back on the field. Dez Bryant was deep for Dallas. I fought off the guy trying to block me and raced after Bryant from the opposite side of the field. Just as I was getting close to him, I felt a pop in my right hamstring. Bryant went 62 yards for a touchdown, and I was now hurt for the second time in my rookie year. We beat Dallas and were now 2-0, but the trainers diagnosed me with a second-degree strain. I was done for three to four weeks. *This could become an injury that nags your whole career. You can't rush it.*

One of the ways we treated my injury was with a platelet-rich plasma shot (or PRP), which encourages healing and reduces inflammation. Still, I ended up sitting out five weeks. Staying locked in as a rookie while not playing was challenging. Coach Byrd kept me involved as best he could. Each week, I had homework that consisted of putting together a scouting report on the opposing tight ends and running backs. I studied how the tight ends ran their routes, if they were quick out of their breaks or used their strength to their advantage. For the backs, I analyzed what type of runners we were facing. Were they fast and shifty? Or were they power backs who liked to run downhill? Even if I wasn't on the field, at least I was learning something that I could use once I was playing again.

I finally returned to action in November. By that time, our record was 4-3. Our next game was in Buffalo against the Bills. The plan was to ease me back into a rotation with Chris Harris and Daniel Manning. I got a total of 15 snaps in our 22-19 victory. I could have played more, but I trusted the coaches and training staff.

Sitting at 5-3, we hosted the Minnesota Vikings the following week. A win would put us in first place in our division. With so much on the line, it felt great when I started getting more reps on defense. When I was hurt, it was like a cloud was hanging over my head. Now, being back with my teammates made me appreciate them and the game a little bit more.

The day of the Minnesota game was freezing cold. As a Florida boy, this was shocking to me. I arrived at Soldier Field extra early because I had to make sure I was good and warmed up. I hit the hot tub, got stretched, and then went outside and did some running. As I was getting dressed in the locker room, I put layers on my arms and legs. I didn't want to feel cold at all. Then Urlacher pulled me aside. *Rook, you are a part of the Bears defense. We don't wear any sleeves here.*

I looked around. For sure, no defensive player had sleeves, so I took mine off. Of course, I was shivering throughout the team warm-up, but I didn't let that get in the way of me doing my job. We won handily over the Vikings, 27-13. My playing time jumped to 25 snaps. I got a big thrill when I tackled Adrian Peterson, one of the best backs in the league.

Up next were the Dolphins in Miami. I was super pumped because my family members and friends would get a chance to see me play in person. I had my best game to date in a 16-0 win. That pushed our record to 7-3, and we maintained our lead in our division.

After two more victories, we prepared for Tom Brady and the New England Patriots. What a rush to play against the quarterback I considered to be the greatest ever! I had been watching Brady on TV for a very long time and really wanted to see in person how good he was. I was thoroughly impressed, especially with his understanding of situational football.

With less than two minutes before halftime, the Patriots got the ball on our 40-yard-line. On the first snap, they ran a side pocket with the tight end sprinting down the middle of the field. This route will always beat cover 2 if the corner doesn't redirect the receiver, and the receiver and the tight end are on the same level. Brady saw exactly what our secondary was doing, and then took advantage of my over-aggressiveness as a rookie. He pump faked to the tight end, which moved me out of position, and hit the receiver in the side pocket for a touchdown. Our coaches cursed me out for allowing a score right before the half. My mistake was that I didn't take the game situation into account. It only added to a very long and frustrating game. The Patriots dog-walked us in a 36-7 blowout. Afterwards, I had even more respect for Brady.

The only good thing about an embarrassing loss is how you respond to it. We had the Vikings in Minnesota up next. This game was huge because the division title was within our reach and we could clinch a spot in the playoffs. Man, all week in practice, things were fun for all the vets. But I was still a step behind. I simply wasn't playing fast enough. I continued working with Coach Byrd to get up to speed.

The city of Minneapolis weathered a nasty snowstorm the week before we arrived. It was so bad that the roof of the Metrodome caved in, which moved our game to the University of Minnesota. It was brutally cold on game day, but I had become somewhat used to it. We were all over the Vikings from the opening kickoff to the last seconds of the game, and won 40-14. Clinching a postseason spot in my first season filled me with joy.

This game was also notable because I was flagged for the first time for helmet-to-helmet contact on a quarterback. I received a letter from the NFL that included a $16,000 fine. I was at a loss for words. *How the hell am I going to pay this?*

The energy at our facility was sky high, but I was way down. When word got around about my fine, all the vets on defense rallied around me and started a pot to help me cover it. That gesture raised my spirits. My teammates had my back, and I felt even closer to them.

With two games left in the regular season, we were focused on getting healthy for the playoffs. We squeaked out a 38-34 win in a dogfight with the New York Jets. Then it was a grudge match against our division rivals, the Green Bay Packers. They gave us everything we could handle in a 10-3 loss. The game had a playoff atmosphere, so it was good preparation for us nonetheless.

We finished the regular season at 11-5, and geared up to host the Seattle Seahawks in the first round of the playoffs. They never really stood a chance. We beat them, 35-24, to set up a rematch with the Packers. This was our third time facing them in 2010, so it was going to be one to remember. Unfortunately, our memories wouldn't be good ones. We lost, 21-14, ending our season on a sour note. I finished my rookie year with 21 tackles (17 solos and 4 assists). Not the production I was hoping for, but it was still a great start for me to build on.

After the season, I went back home to Florida to be with my family, and get my mind and body ready for the 2011 season. I was also on edge for shocking news. A woman back in Chicago was pregnant with my first child. We had met at a club one night, hooked up and we hung out a few times after that.

My first reaction to her pregnancy was so defensive. I cursed her out, called her every bad name I could think of and even made up some new curse words. I was angry because she said she was on birth control. I was dumb enough to believe her. I wasn't ready to be a father. I barely knew how to take care of myself. *How was I going to take care of a kid?*

I also wondered how in the hell I would tell my mother. I knew I had let her down. I told my mom when she was in Chicago after our playoff loss to the Packers. She was speechless, and started to cry. She asked by who, and I admitted that it was a woman who I hardly knew. I said I was scared and sorry. My mom offered me nothing but love and support. *I'm here for you and your child.*

My baby was due in the spring. The mother asked if she could stay in my apartment because it was close to her job. I was hesitant at first, but I knew this would be better for her and the baby, so I agreed. When I told my mom, she was mad. *Son, why would you let a woman you don't know stay in your place? She's going to be going through all your stuff.*

That March I misplaced my wallet and had to cancel my bankcards. All the replacements were to be sent to my place in Chicago. That's when my mom proved to be right again. I called the woman carrying my baby, telling her I had some important mail coming to my house and to overnight it to me when it would get there. But instead, she took my bank debit card. One early morning, I got a call from her crying, telling me she had used my card at the casino and asked me to forgive her. I lost it and told her to get out of my apartment. She refused, which just got me more upset. After cancelling this card, I found out she went to the Horseshoe Casino and ran up more than $2,000 in charges.

I was honestly hurt to my core and didn't know what to do. My mom wanted me to press charges. But the baby was due any day, so that seemed like a bad move. Instead, we flew back to Chicago to handle the situation in person. No one was in the apartment when we got there. I went to the police to find out if I had any options. We decided it wasn't worth it to pursue any legal actions.

A short time later, on April 21, my beautiful daughter, Maliyah Bethany Wright, was born. She was tiny, weighing just 5lbs. 6 ounces. I named her after the great singer, Aaliyah, with an M at the front just like my name.

Holding Maliyah in my hands felt priceless. Before this, I felt like I was being drugged through hell. She changed my life. With responsibilities and obligations to fulfill, I couldn't be selfish anymore. I now had to focus on the upcoming season.

CHAPTER 11
DRIVEN TO DISTRACTION

*Control the things you can control and keep God close,
because the devil is always working nearby.*

Coach Gil Byrd gave me that advice in my second season, during a really tough period for me off the field. As a professional athlete, distractions come at you from all directions. If you're not careful, they can poison your reputation and affect your play negatively. In the NFL, that's suicide for your career. You need to constantly focus on your job.

The week after my daughter was born, the Bears drafted another safety, Chris Conte. Chris Harris, who had been a mentor to me, had left for Carolina as a free agent. Daniel Manning did the same, signing a deal with the Houston Texans. That meant a starting job was waiting for me.

I have to admit that I didn't have a good off-season. It was stressful and mentally draining, and took its toll. When I reported to training camp in late July, I was over my weight by 2lbs. I wasn't allowed to participate in team activities until I got down to 204.

It turned out to be water weight, which I dropped after working out.

My goals heading into 2011 were to stay healthy and show increased production on the field. The media had labeled me as injury prone, and I wanted to prove them wrong. Staying focused wasn't easy because of the drama in my personal life. On one occasion, I was feeling lucky and went to Rivers Casino to do some gambling. While I was shooting dice, I saw the mother of my daughter. She approached me and asked for money. I told her that I was not an ATM, which made her mad. When she started to argue with me, I cashed in my chips and left the casino. As the valet pulled up in my truck, I noticed my right back tire was going flat. I put on my blinking lights and drove slowly to a gas station. Seconds later, guess who pulled up beside me?

At this point, all I wanted to do was put air in my tire and go home. But this woman who I shared my daughter with wanted to continue her argument from the casino. I tried to diffuse the situation, telling her that we had nothing to talk about. She wouldn't quit, so I decided to go inside the gas station and call the police. In doing so, I moved her and her arm out of my way.

When the police showed up, they split us up and talked to her first. An officer came to me and said she was accusing me of hitting her. I lost my breath for a second. Then I regained my composure. *Officer, I was the one who called the police. I was trying to prevent a fight from happening.*

But at this point the whole situation was turned upside-down. The officers talked to her again, and then reported to me that *she* didn't want to press charges. It was crazy. I asked the officer how I was supposed to stay out of trouble if calling the police led to more of it. He told me to avoid situations that put me in bad positions. I was so mad. This chick was trying to make me lose my dream job, something I had worked hard for my whole life. I was so hot I could barely see driving. I called our team security guy, Tom Dillon, and told him everything that happened. He was in disbelief. *Go home and don't do anything that you'll regret. We will talk about this in the morning.*

The next day, when I got to our facility, Coach Smith called me into his office. He asked what happened the night before. I explained everything to him. He responded that I had to be more careful, especially around the mother of my daughter. These types of problems weren't good for my career or the Bears. Coach Smith had heard about a similar experience, so he knew what I was going through. His advice was to make sure a third party was around whenever my girl's mother and I had to interact. From that day forward, that's exactly what I did.

Blocking out distractions like this can be hard. In practice that day, I made three mental errors, all because my mind was not in the right place. I couldn't let this put my career in jeopardy.

Our 2011 season opened against the New Orleans Saints at the Superdome. It was one of the loudest games I have played as a pro. We tried to simulate the noise in practice, but nothing compared to the real deal. We didn't handle it well, and got beat, 30-13. I left the game early with a concussion, the first of my career. I was forced to sit out the next two games, which only added to the perception of me being injury prone.

After our loss to the Saints, we rebounded and won five of our next seven games. I recovered from my concussion and was cleared to play. Finally, I felt like I was getting into a rhythm on the field. Then, in early November, I got a phone call that provided a new distraction. I didn't recognize the number, but my gut told me to answer it. It was the Cook County Police Department. *Mr. Wright, we need you to come pick up your daughter.*

I rushed out my house worried for my 6 months old daughter. When I got to the police station, Maliyah was screaming at the top of her lungs and crying. I called Rhonda Byrd, who was working as my assistant, and asked for help. She and her best friend Monica met me back at my place. We were up with Maliyah until 3:30 in the morning because she wouldn't stop crying. I had to be at the facility at 8am, and I was drained physically and emotionally. When Coach Byrd saw me, he knew something wasn't right. He could see it on my face. After telling him what happened, he took me to our meeting room and we prayed together. He gave me a great advice, *control the things you can control and keep God close, because the devil is always working nearby*

Later during meetings, Rhonda texted me that Maliyah had been picked up by her mother. She was very rude to her, snatched the baby out of her arms, gave her the stank look, and didn't even say thank you. In the midst of all this, I had to prepare for our game against the Detroit Lions and their high-powered offense. That Sunday, Coach Byrd asked if I was mentally ready. *I'ma show you, coach.*

The previous week, I had picked off Michael Vick. They say interceptions come in bunches, so I was expecting another against Detroit. We burst out to a 14-0 lead on a 6-yard touchdown by Matt Forte and an 82-yard punt return by Devin Hester. In the second half, the Lions had to throw the ball to get back in the game. With the ball on their 20-yard-line, we got into a cover 3 defense. That means 3 deep and 4 under zone. My responsibility was anything in the flats. On the snap, I saw the tight end going to the flat and Matthew Stafford looking right at him. I jumped the route as he released the ball, intercepted the pass and returned it 24 yards for a touchdown. It was the first pick-6 of my NFL career. As I crossed the goal line, I had one thought. *What am I going to do now?*

I'm known as a good dancer, but I had really never practiced a touchdown celebration. I ended up doing something called the "Elroy," which Tim Jennings taught me earlier in the week. I'm not sure I pulled out my best moves, but I was super crunk and the fans loved it. On the next series, Charles Tillman got a pick-6 of his own. We went on to beat Detroit, 37-13.

From there, we really struggled and finished the season without making the playoffs at 8-8. I started 12 games and racked up 58 tackles. I also had three interceptions. Still, given all the off-field drama, I was happy with my second season in the NFL.

Going into my third season, I made it a priority to take care of my body and put the work in during the off-season. I also did my best to tune out all the noise in my personal life. It helped when I changed back to my old number. Corey Graham had signed with the Baltimore Ravens, which made #21 available. I grabbed it immediately. I felt like that number made me play better. Without a doubt, it gave me more swag. I reported to training camp in great shape. My body fat was just 10%, the lowest it had ever been.

I set a few goals for 2012. One was to pick off Peyton Manning. My chance came when we faced the Denver Broncos in the preseason. This was huge in my eyes because Manning was a future Hall of

Famer. Intercepting him would give me bragging rights the rest of my life. I got my pick in the first half, and then cut my day short when I felt a little tightness in my hamstring. The "old me" would have played through it. The "new me" was mature enough to back off.

We raced out to a great start, winning three of our first four games. I already had three interceptions, two off Tony Romo and a pick-6 off Sam Bradford. Our defense was having so much fun. We were ranked in top 5 in every category, including #1 in turnovers. Everything was a competition in the secondary. We made a wager that the player with the most interceptions would win $1,000 from each of the guys playing regular snaps. There were six of us in all, so not a bad payday.

After 10 games, we were 8-2. Special teams, offense and defense were all clicking, and I was playing my best ball. Chicago offered me a three-year contract extension at $6 million. I felt I was worth way more than that, so I turned it down.

Meanwhile, we were getting ready to host the Seahawks. Our fans at Soldier Field had been outstanding all year. They were so loud at times we had to use hand signals to communicate in the secondary. We expected much the same for Seattle.

The game was tight into to the fourth quarter. We led 14-10 with time running out. The Seahawks had the ball on their 31-yard-line, and came out in a spread formation. We were in cover 2. On the snap, our pass rush was all over Russell Wilson, who lofted a pass down the middle of the field. I broke on the ball and went up with two hands but dropped what would have been the game-winning interception. I lay on the ground, screaming at myself for not making the play. Seattle took advantage and drove 69 yards to win 17-14. I felt so bad knowing I let my brothers down.

That loss sent us into a tailspin. We lost our next two games before beating the Arizona Cardinals. We now needed a win over Detroit on the final Sunday of the year to make the playoffs. Unfortunately, we weren't up to the challenge. The Lions beat us with a late touchdown, leaving us at 10-6 and out of the post-season. Not making the playoffs really cut me deep. I felt like it was my fault, because of my missed interception against the Seahawks. Not a day went by when I didn't think about that play.

Still, there was no doubt I had my best season. I started all 16 games, recording 71 tackles (including five for a loss), four interceptions, two fumble recoveries, and one forced fumble. I was named an alternate for the Pro Bowl. I was proud of my how far I had come, but I also knew there was room for improvement.

Tim Jennings ultimately took home the wager prize of $6,000 with a league-leading nine interceptions.

When it came time for our exit meetings, something just wasn't right. Coach Smith addressed us as a team, and then told us he had been fired. It was shocking news to everybody. I wondered if I was somehow responsible.

A while later, my agent reached out to the Bears to talk about a new contract. They told him that I wasn't a priority. I decided to use that as motivation for the 2013 season, the last of my four-year contract. But there was also some uncertainty. *Had I been smart to turn down the extension offer?*

Clearly the Bears were moving in a new direction. They hired Marc Trestman as the new head coach, and Mel Tucker was named the defensive coordinator. The biggest news came when they cut Brian Urlacher. It was more shocking than the firing of Coach Smith. Urlacher was the leader of our defense, not to mention the best defensive player I have ever played with. He was so smart. He could tell you the play before the offense snapped the ball. He made everyone on defense better.

Urlacher was also a great person. When I was drafted, he welcomed me with open arms. I'm not going to lie. When I first met him, I thought he was going to be a dickhead. But he was the most amazing guy; great personality and kind-hearted. A family man who loved having fun and would go to war for his team.

With Urlacher gone, management was making a statement. We all heard it loud and clear. No one was safe.

CHAPTER 12

THE END ZONE

*I kept hoping to get another call. I was watching every
NFL game to see if any safeties got hurt.*

It's sad to say, but that's where I was by the end of my career. I wasn't exactly rooting for an injury to a safety out there. I just wanted another opportunity. It was hard to admit that I was done.

Going into the fourth and final year of my contract, I was in a great space. Despite some bumps in the road, I was focused on playing my best football. Even though we had a new coaching staff in Chicago, everything stayed the same on defense: play fast and be physical.

We won our first two games of the 2013 season, and then faced the Pittsburgh Steelers in a Sunday night showdown. We won, 40-23, and I played great with seven tackles, a forced fumble, and an interception that I returned 38 yards for a touchdown. I was rewarded for my efforts by being named defensive player of the game. What an amazing feeling—preparing for a team and executing just as you envisioned it.

Unfortunately, we got hit with the injury bug. Midway through the season, only five of our 11 starters on defense were healthy. We went from a top five unit to damn near last in the league. Some of the guys the Bears brought in as replacements had literally been sitting on their couches at home. We couldn't stop the run. We weren't getting any pressure on the quarterback. It was a recipe for disaster. We finished the season at 8-8 and nowhere close to playoffs. I led the team in tackles with 100, and also had two interceptions (one returned for a touchdown), two forced fumbles, and two fumble recoveries.

I felt my fourth season was a great year. The Bears didn't agree. When my agent approached them about a new contract, they said they wanted to go in a different direction. Hearing that news crushed my heart. It made me hate the Chicago organization. It wasn't simply because they didn't want to re-sign me, but also because I had made the Windy City my second home. I knew I was going to miss everything about it, even those brutally cold winters.

As a free agent, I wasn't sure where I would land next. I really wanted to go to a team in Chicago's division, just so I could play them twice a year. But Lovie Smith had just been hired as the head coach of the Tampa Bay Buccaneers. He wanted me to come along and build what we had in Chicago. This wasn't an easy decision because they had two great safeties, Mark Barron and Dashon Goldson. I knew if I signed with the Bucs, I would have to earn my way on the field. But after weighing all my options, I determined that Tampa was the best fit. I signed a one-year deal for the veteran minimum of $795,000. I bet on myself because I knew what I was capable of doing in Coach Smith's system.

I felt pressure for sure. It reminded of what it was like when I was a kid, moving from town to town and having to prove myself to new coaches and teammates. I had always overcome those obstacles. *Why would I stop doing that now?*

The Tampa roster was full of second and third-year players. It was a little weird being called an "old head." Coach Smith explained my role to me. I would play on special teams and rotate in on defense. This took me back to my rookie year. As I mentioned, I was cool with the idea of proving myself because I had been doing it my whole life.

Then, a little less than halfway through the 2014 season, Tampa traded Barron to the Rams. That opened a starting job for me. I was grateful for the opportunity, but as a team we were terrible. We finished at 4-12, tied for last in our division. I started seven games and recorded 51 tackles. That was my lowest output since my rookie season. But my bigger concern was ending the year on injured reserve with hurt ribs.

In the off-season, the Bucs offered me a new contract: two years at $2.5 million, with the first year fully guaranteed. I could make an extra $1.5 million with incentives. All this was motivation for me to go hard. Not too long after I signed my deal, Tampa cut Goldson. He was one of my good friends on the team, so I was sorry to see him go. The Bucs brought in DJ Swearinger as well as one of my old teammates, Chris Conte. We already had Keith Tandy and Bradley McDougald, so depth was not a problem. Coach Smith told us that the safety spot was up for grabs. We were all competing for the same job.

Before our second preseason game that August, I got a phone call at 4:30 in the morning from my mother. She was crying hysterically. I could barely hear what she was saying at first. *Your grandmother*

Major Pain: Confessions of a Smash-Mouth Safety

Carolyn Lee is sick. The doctors say she isn't going to make it through the night.

I instantly broke down. My grandmother was the life of our family. She meant the world to me, and I meant the world to her. She was so proud of all of my accomplishments. She talked about me to anyone who would listen. She would even call me and have me talk to strangers she just met. I always got a text or call from her before games, just to wish me luck.

Now, my grandmother was gone, at the age of 64. I couldn't stop thinking about all the great memories we had together. I loved staying at her house with my uncles. I remember one day when I was about nine, and I was on punishment for bad grades. I decided to show all the kids in the neighborhood that I could do back flips off of my grandmother's roof. I got up on top of the house wearing this bright red shirt. That's when I saw my grandmother driving around the corner in her blue Buick. I quickly jumped down, ran inside the house and changed my shirt. Then I met her in the front yard, and helped her carry things inside. She asked if I had seen anyone on the roof in a red shirt. I showed her my black shirt and answered no. Of course, she already knew the truth. *Boy, you thought I was born yesterday, I knew that was you on the roof the whole time.*

The Bucs were great about the whole thing. They got me on the first plane home, and Coach Smith told me to spend as much time as I needed with my family. After a few days, I returned to Tampa because I knew I had a job I was fighting for, and I wanted to play in our final preseason game against the Miami Dolphins. My grandmother wouldn't have had it any other way. I had an outstanding game, recording seven tackles and an interception.

I used that momentum to carry me into the 2015 season. We opened against the Tennessee Titans. I reset my mind back to my college days, when I was playing recklessly and with full force. On our first series on defense, I came downhill and dropped the boom on a Tennessee running back. The crowd went wild, but I got flagged for a penalty. At that moment, I realized the game of football had changed. Making receivers pay for catching the ball was my specialty. It was hard to be taught one thing and then go against your instincts.

I knew my hit against the Titans was clean, but the NFL didn't see it that way. I grew up playing football very violently, always intent on destroying any man across from me. I understood that the league was trying to make football safer now, but what it was asking from defenders was almost impossible. The game is played at such high speeds. Unless you're playing two-hand touch, avoiding dangerous hits is unrealistic. And as a defensive player, the risk of getting injured is more likely when you have to hesitate to make that perfect tackle. When you can't lead with your head or shoulders, it's more like you're taking the blow than delivering it.

I was on the *receiving* end of a hard hit later in the Tennessee game. I got a knee to my back, leaving me almost unable to walk. I had a knot the size of a tennis ball, which sidelined me for a few weeks. I returned for our game against the New Orleans Saints. But the injury bug bit me again. This time it was tightness in my hamstring. I stayed in the game, finishing with eight tackles and two pass deflections in a 24-17 loss.

Afterward, the trainers looked at me and told me to get a MRI on my knee. I was confused because it felt like it was my hamstring that needed treatment. The news was awful. *You have a torn meniscus.*

I couldn't believe it. For the second season in a row, I ended up on injury reserve. Even worse, I needed to have surgery to repair the damage to my knee. A short time later, Coach Smith was fired. I was at a loss for words. I was also worried about what was next for me.

In January of 2016, the Bucs named Dirk Koetter as their new head coach. Mike Smith was hired as the defensive coordinator. Meanwhile, my rehab was going great. As OTAs approached, I was starting to get my strength and range of motion back. The team workouts were incredibly intense, not only physically but also mentally. We had to learn more than 60 new defensive schemes, including code words and signals. It was overwhelming at first.

Going into training camp, I wasn't as confident as my previous seasons. Under the new system, it was their way or the highway. I wasn't interested in losing my job, so on the first day we put on pads, I decided it was only right that I set the tone. When the offense ran a toss, I squared up the running back and put a nice lick on him. The defense got crunk! The next play, I dropped the boom on a tight end and forced a pass breakup. I was on fire, but a rain delay moved us inside for about 45 minutes. When it was time to go back out, Coach Koetter came to me. *Major, you're done for the rest of the day. See you tomorrow.*

I was stunned. Coach Koetter explained that my hit on the tight end was illegal and would have drawn a fine from the league. The next day, the coaches showed me clips of my plays. I was told the first hit was great, but the one on the tight end was a cheap shot. I honestly didn't agree but kept it to myself. It was all very confusing. *Isn't this the kind of physical play you want from your safety?*

As we were getting ready for our preseason opener against the Philadelphia Eagles, I began to feel soreness in my surgically repaired right knee. I tried telling myself that it was just fatigue. All I needed was to ice it. When it continued to bother me, I got treatment on my own. The trainers noticed me limping around and asked if I was hurting. I told them I was fine, but in the back of my mind I was concerned. I played against Philadelphia, though it was clear that I wasn't at 100 percent. A few days later I got a call from a Tampa area code. I knew what was up immediately. The Bucs cut me. It wasn't a surprise.

As soon I got cut, my agent called to say that he had scheduled a workout with the Carolina Panthers. I was still in a lot of pain, but I had to show up because there was no predicting if and when another opportunity would come. I called Dr. Casey Ho, one of the best sports medicine chiropractor out of Houston, and flew to Texas to get worked on. That gave me some peace of mind, but I wasn't anywhere close to be being fully healthy.

I arrived in Charlotte a few nights later, and was up until 1am filling out a large packet of information. My day started five hours later. The team sent a car to pick me up, and my first stop was the doctor's office for my physical. I handed my packet to the doctor. He frowned as he flipped through it. Then he started asking about my knee. Apparently, I had missed a form and he wondered if I was trying to hide something. I told him it was an honest mistake, but there was something weird in the way he looked at me.

When I got to the Carolina facility, they gave me my workout gear and told me to get dressed in a bathroom. While in there, I gave myself a shot of a painkiller known as Toradol. They walked me out to the field, as the Panthers were finishing practice. A few of the guys came over to talk and wish me good luck. It felt so good being back on the field.

I went out and killed my workout. My only thought after was where was I going to stay in Charlotte when the Panthers signed me. I took a shower and then met with some of the coaches. Next, they told me to wait for a meeting with head Coach Ron Rivera and general manager Dave Gettleman. When I sat down with them, they said my workout went great, but there was an issue with my physical. The doctor claimed that I wouldn't cooperate with him. I couldn't believe what I just heard. *I'm here to get a job. Do you really think I wouldn't comply with him? That's not how I do things.*

I spent the next 45 minutes waiting on their decision. I texted my agent, asking if he had heard anything. Finally, they told me the bad news. They weren't offering me a contract. This broke my heart. I almost cried right there.

A week later, I got a call from the Lions to work out for them. But this was just to see what type of shape I was in, not necessarily to sign a deal. I had a great workout but nothing happened. The Dolphins called me a week after that. Everything went smooth, but I wasn't their guy. They signed another safety instead.

In November, the Bucs called and re-signed me after one of their safeties went down. I was so happy. I was willing to do whatever they asked. I played in two games, and then Tampa cut me again. I felt so used and lost. To add insult to injury, they timed the move so that I wouldn't get credit for playing in a seventh NFL season.

I had to come to grips with the fact that my football career might be over. The sport had opened so many doors for me. Now, after 20 years of blood, sweat, and tears, it appeared to be done, just like that. It was hard to process, and I struggled to deal with it. I was angry and depressed. Letting go of the sport I loved would take time, and I now had plenty of it. Eventually, I embraced the challenge of starting a new life for myself.

In retrospect, I'm so grateful for the game of football. I'm especially grateful for the friendships I built, all my brothers I went to war with, and all of the amazing fans who supported me. Saying good-bye is hard. But it's made easier when you feel thankful from the bottom of your heart. Football taught me so many life skills. The most important is the knowledge that there is nothing on this earth I can't do. I can't think of a better way to live my life. Football may be out of the equation for me, but that drive to be successful will never leave

EPILOGUE

I've learned throughout my life that if you surround yourself with positive energy, keep positive thoughts and are consistent in whatever it is you want to achieve, nothing can get in your way—except yourself.

This might be the most important lesson from all my years of football. I think I knew it all along, but it became crystal clear after my career ended. My life was crashing down all around me. I was lost, and couldn't get out of my own way.

I didn't give up on my career immediately. In fact, after being cut for the second time by Tampa, I continued to work out faithfully, hoping that I would get another call soon. A few months went by and my lease in Tampa was up, so I moved back home to Fort Lauderdale with my mother. At the time I needed all the support I could get. I felt like I wasn't good enough and even questioned myself as a person.

I fought hard to get through all the doubts, and tried my best to stay ready. But I found myself sleeping more and more. I wasn't motivated to do much at all. I really had a hard time understanding that football couldn't be my whole life anymore. *What else am I good at? Is football it?*

OTAs started in the spring of 2017, and I didn't receive one call. I told myself that teams wouldn't be interested in me until camp at the end of July. As we moved deeper into the summer, I started calling my agent regularly to see if I got any invites. The answer was always the same. My hopes of getting back in the league were seriously fading. Meanwhile, my bills were piling up. Having no income was taking a toll on me mentally. The season passed, and I was still jobless.

I approached 2018 with the same mentality—I would not give up on football. I was going to work extra hard this time around. In March, I flew to Los Angeles to join Joe Haden. He could push me harder than anyone, and I could do the same for him. We did that all the way up in until May, when players had to report for OTAs. I convinced myself that I would be picked up this time for sure. I was in tip-top shape and feeling better mentally. But the call never came.

At this point in my life, I was finally ready to face the truth: football was over for me. I would have never imagined in a million years that my career would have ended so quietly, with me playing in two games in 2016 and not even completing a full season.

I felt helpless. For once in my life, I had no answer. Having no income for several years sucked up all my funds, which led to even more stress. I had to go to court to try to reduce my child support payments because I couldn't afford the $3,700 a month that I had agreed to years earlier. Things got so bad that my car was repossessed.

I tried going back to school, but quickly grew frustrated with it. I had fell into a very dark place. I asked a bunch of friends for favors, but none of them could fix my long-term problem, finding steady income. I had heard about so many athletes going broke after football. *Was I really going to be one of them?*

So here I was, stuck in this suffocating downward spiral, which brings me back to the start of this book. When my Line of Duty Disability came in, I felt like I reached a turning point. Today, I couldn't be happier with my life. I've got so many good things going on. I live with the same mentality I embraced when I was playing football. I just know there is nothing that's going to stop me from becoming even better than before. But that's a story for my next book. Mark my words. *It will be so inspiring!*

Middle School

Tallahassee

High School

High School Action

Signing Day

UNIVERSITY OF FLORIDA

February 8, 2006

Major Wright
c/o Coach George Smith
St. Thomas Aquinas High School
2801 Southwest 12th Street
Fort Lauderdale, FL 33312

Dear Major,

We have just finished with the #1 recruiting class in the nation. The enthusiasm and excitement of **Florida Gator Football** has spread throughout the **Gator Nation**.

You are a great safety, one who will bring excitement to the 92,000 **Gator** fans at **"The Swamp."** Blessed with great talent, you will have an immediate impact when you set foot on the field.

The **University of Florida** is one of the elite institutions in the world. As a member of the Association of American Universities, a prestigious higher education organization of only the top universities in the United States, the **University of Florida** offers 100 undergraduate degree programs to students from all over the world. We are the only school to belong to this prestigious organization and have its football team ranked in the Top 25 over the last 16 years.

This letter is written as a **full football scholarship** to the **University of Florida** beginning with the 2007 academic year.

The **University of Florida** is a great institution both on and off the field. You will grow in stature as a man both on and off the field at the **University of Florida**.

We need you to join the **University of Florida** "Football Family." My door is always open. My personal cell phone number is 352-317-3711.

Remember- when you visit **"The Swamp,"** only the **Gators** get out alive!

Sincerely,

Urban Meyer
Head Football Coach
University of Florida

High School

Alligator Newspaper

University of Florida

Pro Day

Draft Day

Chicago Bears

Tampa Bay Buccaneers

THANK YOU

God.

My Mother Andrea Eluett and my father Major Wright.

My grandmothers Carolyn Lee and Daisy Wright. My Grandfather Harry Wright. My Auntie Ella Dulcio. My uncles Malcom Lewis and Chris Lee. My cousins Jessica Mann, James Demetric and Nick Dulcio. My sisters Alexis Bryant, Bryanna Wright, Charity Wright, Tatyanna Wright and Yasmine Jones. My brothers Daniel Wright and Majon Wright.

Coach Cris Carter. Melanie Carter and their kids Duron and Monterae.

Marie Alves and my auntie Lois Eluett

And all the other members of my family.

The Western Tigers, The Lauderdale Lakes Vikings and the Pine Hills Trojans.

Corey Baillow, and all of my friends in Orlando and Tallahassee.

My neighborhood friends, Jeffery Harris, Chad, Keith, Kevin, Kevin McCaskill and their parents.

My Nims middle school friends Clint, Glenn Stanley and Charmaine, and all of my other Nims middle school friends.

My Nims middle school teachers, Ms Richardson and Ms Mia Thomas.

Godby high school teachers, classmates, friends. My teammate DeAndre McDaniel.

My St. Thomas Aquinas high school friends, Bobby Crawford, Richard Goodman, Stanley Gaston, Chris Reed, Jeffery Fuller and Leonard Hankerson. Ms. Bom my tutor at St. Thomas Aquinas.

My UF teammates, Joe Haden, Ahmad Black, Moses Jenkins, Lorenzo Edwards, Carlos Dunlap, Deontae Thomson, Chris Rainy, Markihe Anderson, Ryan Stamper, Brandon James, Brandon Spikes, Tim Tebow and Percy Harvey.

The University of Florida, teachers, Crystal my tutor, classmates and all of my friends in Gainesville, Florida.

My agents Mitch Frankie of Impact Sports and Sean Kiernan. My trainer Tony Villani of XPE Sports.

My Chicago Bears teammates, Brian Urlacker, Tim Jennings, Charles Tillman, Henry Melton, Chris Conte, JT Thomas, Devin Hester, Julies Pepper and Chris Harris.

The Chicago Bears organization, the GM Jerry Angelo, the training staff, doctors, and strength staff.

Perry and all of my friends in Chicago. Laisha Fox my ex-girlfriend.

My Tampa Bay teammates, Gerald Willams, Vontae David, Dashon Goldson, Mike Evans, and Russel Shepard.

The Tampa Bay Buccaneers organization, the training staff, doctors, and strength staff.

My Coaches at Western Tigers.

Coach Fred, Coach Walt, Coach Chris and every other coaches at Lauderdale Lakes.

My coaches at Pine Hills Trojans.

Coach Cedric Gaines and Coach Troy at Nims middle school.

My Coaches at Godby high school, Coach Cruise, Coach Mike, Coach Jesse Forbes, Coach Todd Lantern.

Coach George Smith, Coach Shepherd, Coach Conley, Coach Spence, Coach Castillo, Coach Alex Armenteros and Coach Simmons at St. Thomas Aquinas high school.

Coach Urban Myers, Coach Doc Holliday, Coach Chuck Heater, Coach Vance Bedford, and Coach Charlie Strong at University of Florida.

Mike Kennedy my book editor, Joel Crayton my book designer, Mike Perez my photographer and Cat Peoples for advising me on process of getting my book published.

And if we have ever crossed paths and you inspired me in any way, thank you!

Major Wright is a retired football player who attended the University of Florida from 2007 to 2009. He led the SEC in fumbles and was named a First-Team Freshman All-American at UF. He was a member of the 2008 National Championship winning team.

He was picked by the Chicago Bears in the third round of the 2010 NFL draft. He played four years for the Chicago Bears and two years with the Tampa Bay Buccaneers.

He is currently living in Miami, Florida. 'Major Pain: Confessions of a Smash-Mouth Safety' is his first book.

www.majorwright.com
Twitter: @lilmade21
Instagram: @lilmade21
Snapchat: lilmade21
Facebook: lilmade21

Major Wright

Made in the USA
Columbia, SC
09 June 2020